MESSAGE OF THE FATHERS OF THE CHURCH

DEATH

AND

RESURRECTION

by

Joanne E. McWilliam Dewart

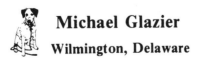

Michael Glazier
Wilmington, Delaware

ABOUT THE AUTHOR

JOANNE E. McWILLIAM DEWART received her doctorate in theology from the University of St. Michael's College in Toronto. She has written and lectured widely on theological, philosophical and patristic topics, and her published works indicate her expertise in the thought of the Fathers of the Church.

First published in 1986 by Michael Glazier, Inc.
1935 West Fourth Steet, Wilmington, Delaware 19805

Distributed outside U.S., Canada, Australia, and Philippines by Geoffrey Chapman, a division of Cassel Ltd., 1 Vincent Square, London SWIP 2PN.

Library of Congress Catalog Card Number: 85-45560
International Standard Book Number:
Message of the Fathers of the Church series:
  (0-89453-312-6, Paper; 0-89453-340-1, Cloth)
DEATH & RESURRECTION
  (0-89453-333-9, Paper)
  (0-89453-362-2, Cloth)

Cover design: Lillian Brulc

Typography by Debbie L. Farmer

Printed in the United States

CONTENTS

Editor's Introduction

The *Message of the Fathers of the Church* is a companion series to The *Old Testament Message* and The *New Testament Message*. It was conceived and planned in the belief that Scripture and Tradition worked hand in hand in the formation of the thought, life and worship of the primitive Church. Such a series, it was felt, would be a most effective way of opening up what has become virtually a closed book to present-day readers, and might serve to stimulate a revival in interest in Patristic studies in step with the recent, gratifying resurgence in Scriptural studies.

The term "Fathers" is usually reserved for Christian writers marked by orthodoxy of doctrine, holiness of life, ecclesiastical approval and antiquity. "Antiquity" is generally understood to include writers down to Gregory the Great (+604) or Isidore of Seville (+636) in the West, and John Damascene (+749) in the East. In the present series, however, greater elasticity has been encouraged, and quotations from writers not noted for orthodoxy will sometimes be included in order to illustrate the evolution of the Message on particular doctrinal matters. Likewise, writers later than the mid-eighth century will sometimes be used to illustrate the continuity of tradition on matters like sacramental theology or liturgical practice.

An earnest attempt was made to select collaborators on a broad inter-disciplinary and inter-confessional basis, the chief consideration being to match scholars who could handle the Fathers in their original languages with subjects in which they had already demonstrated a special interest and competence. About the only editorial directive given to the

7

selected contributors was that the Fathers, for the most part, should be allowed to speak for themselves and that they should speak in readable, reliable modern English. Volumes on individual themes were considered more suitable than volumes devoted to individual Fathers, each theme, hopefully, contributing an important segment to the total mosaic of the Early Church, one, holy, catholic and apostolic. Each volume has an introductory essay outlining the historical and theological development of the theme, with the body of the work mainly occupied with liberal citations from the Fathers in modern English translation and a minimum of linking commentary. Short lists of Suggested Further Readings are included; but dense, scholarly footnotes were actively discouraged on the pragmatic grounds that such scholarly shorthand has other outlets and tends to lose all but the most relentlessly esoteric reader in a semipopular series.

At the outset of his *Against Heresies* Irenaeus of Lyons warns his readers "not to expect from me any display of rhetoric, which I have never learned, or any excellence of composition, which I have never practised, or any beauty or persuasiveness of style, to which I make no pretensions." Similarly, modest disclaimers can be found in many of the Greek and Latin Fathers and all too often, unfortunately, they have been taken at their word by an uninterested world. In fact, however, they were often highly educated products of the best rhetorical schools of their day in the Roman Empire, and what they have to say is often as much a lesson in literary and cultural, as well as in spiritual, edification.

St. Augustine, in *The City of God* (19.7), has interesting reflections on the need for a common language in an expanding world community; without a common language a man is more at home with his dog than with a foreigner as far as intercommunication goes, even in the Roman Empire, which imposes on the nations it conquers the yoke of both law and language with a resultant abundance of interpreters. It is hoped that in the present world of continuing language barriers the contributors to this series will prove opportune interpreters of the perennial Christian message.

Thomas Halton

ACKNOWLEDGEMENTS

My thanks are due — and happily given — first to the staff at 47 Queen's Park Crescent East, Toronto, who cheerfully endured my combining administration and writing, secondly to my graduate assistants, Eileen Smith and Daniel Williams, who were tireless in tracking down books and checking references, and, thirdly, to my colleagues, Christopher Ryan and Peter Slater, who read the manuscript through and made many valuable suggestions for its improvement.

INTRODUCTION

The mystery of death has compelled attention since human history was first recorded and it has been said that the existential truth of a religious myth "can be measured... by [its] power to solve... the problem of death."[1] An account of the myths[2] which have surrounded death or an assessment of how much Christianity, its faith founded on Christ's victory over death, owes to these myths is clearly beyond the scope of this study. But it is well to keep in mind, while examining the views of the patristic church on death and resurrection, that no more in this area than in any other did the Christians of the church's first few centuries bring their message to unformed minds; there was already a rich human heritage of eschatological hopes and visions.

Rich and varied as the myths which attempted to penetrate its mystery were, death retained, with its inevitability, its awesome opaqueness. The human spirit, uniquely conscious of self and time, has consistently resisted the prospect of a definitive end, and in the ancient world this resistance found as many expressions as there were cultures. Within

[1] J.S. Dunne, *The City of the Gods: a Study in Myth and Morality* (New York: Macmillan, 1965), v.

[2] I use 'myth' here in the sense of the language of narrative employed to deal with events located beyond historical time and geographical space in an effort to convey their meaning to those living in time and space.

this abundance certain patterns formed: there were efforts to out-manoeuvre death (the story of Gilgamesh), to bridge the gulf between the living and the dead (that of Orpheus), to provide for life beyond the grave (the burying of food and tools in the egyptian pyramids), to find comfort in the recurring renewals of the physical world (the fertility religions, many with rites of sacred marriage) or in the ongoing life of the family (the roman deification of ancestors).

Some of these attempts clearly imply hope of life beyond death, and one finds the "oldest clearly formulated belief"[3] in a happy afterlife for the individual in the egyptian cult of Osiris. In this cult at first the Pharoah alone gained immortality by identification with the ever-living sun. Later the privilege was extended to his people as well. In some other cultures (the greek and indian) the evident mortality of the body prompted belief in what Plato called "the sorrowful weary wheel" of metempsychosis,[4] with its hope of eventual release from the material world (Pythagoreanism). Other cultures, more practically, encouraged participation in disciplines and rites by means of which the soul could discard the body and ascend to the realm of pure spirit immediately after death (Orphism).

To defeat death and attain a happy afterlife was to impinge on the territory of the gods, and so the mystery of death necessarily involved the mystery of the divine. As speculation about the one developed so it did about the other. Particularly in societies where justice was seen to be an attribute of divinity a post-mortem discrimination between those who had lived just or unjust lives became part of the eschatological myth (post-exilic Judaism). Frequently, although not universally, a role was assigned to a mythical saviour who had conquered death and was able

---

[3]S. Croalto, "The Hope of Immortality in the Main Cosmologies of the East," in *Immortality and Resurrection*, eds. P. Benoit and R. Murphy (London: Burns and Oates, 1970), 26.

[4]*Phaedrus* 248-49, quoted S.G.J. Brandon, *The Judgement of the Dead: an Historical and Comparative Study of the Idea of a 'Post Mortem' Judgement in the Major Religions*. (London: Weidenfeld and Nicolson, 1967), 90.

and willing to share that conquest with others (the gnostic divine man).

One of the reasons the christian eschatological hope gained a hearing was that it responded to perennial human fears and hopes, and, because it evoked echoes of other, more ancient responses to those same fears and hopes, it had a certain reassuring familiarity. But there was novelty as well in the christian gospel, above all in its being anchored so tenaciously in history. The dispelling of the fear of death and the secure anticipation of a happy afterlife were rooted in the Christians' claim that already one historical person— the man whose disciples they were—had indeed conquered death and that his victory could be shared. The measure of their success in convincing others of the validity of this eschatological blend of old and new is attested in the rapid spread of Christianity in the face of many competing religions, at a time when it had relatively little to offer in terms of more immediate advantage.

1. THE BACKGROUND

The Old Testament

Because of the jewish matrix from which Christianity emerged, the attempts of the Jews of the Old Testament and of the intertestamental period to deal with death have a special relevance for early christian thinking on the subject. When the Israelites entered Canaan they found an indigenous belief in the recurring renewal of life through the cycle of the earth's seasons, but they repudiated this religion of nature in favour of one based on a monolatrous covenant with their God, revealed in the events of history. The death of the individual was understood as the consequence of sin (Gen 3:19), and for more than a thousand years that sentence was seen to be irrevocable. The Israelites were able to subsume personal death into the ongoing life and welfare of the nation, the welfare which was a witness to divine faithfulness to the covenant. Although this national covenantal bond was increasingly understood not unconditionally, but rather as ethically conditioned, divine justice (like human) was at first seen to deal in terms of families and nations, not of individuals,[1] and to operate in an historical, not in a suprahistorical nor even an eschatological setting.

In this context, the israelite expectation of individual existence (it could hardly be called life) after death could only be that of Sheol, an existence described as one of torpor:[2] "There is no work or thought or knowledge or wisdom in Sheol. . . ."[3] Sheol was sometimes seen as outside divine governance:

> [I am] like one forsaken among the dead,
> like this slain that lie in the grave,
> like those whom thou [Lord] dost remember no more,
> for they are cut off from thy hand";[4]

sometimes it was seen to be within:

> If I ascend to heaven, thou are there!
> If I take up my bed in Sheol, thou art there![5]

In either case Sheol was a condition in which there was little differentiation between just and unjust and from which there was no escape.

It was not only the belief that the divine covenant was with the nation, not the individual, and therefore promised no personal happiness apart from the assurance of the welfare of the nation, which led to the minimalist understanding of Sheol. Equally important was the ancient israelite conviction that no true life was possible without the body, and, consequently, that any existence of the soul separated from the body (as existence in Sheol was envisaged to be) could be merely a pale shadow of real life.

[1]Andre-Marie Dubarle, "Belief in Immortality in the Old Testament and Judaism," in *Immortality and Resurrection*, ed. P. Benoit and R. Murphy (New York: Herder and Herder, 1970), 34.

[2]Dubarle, 38.

[3]Eccl 9:10.

[4]Ps 88:5.

[5]Ps 139:8.

The exile of the sixth century B.C.E. and the events and interpretations surrounding it decisively changed Israel's covenantal self-consciousness, and eventually, after several centuries, these changes were reflected in a new understanding of the human person vis-a-vis the mystery of death. Two of the most important factors which contributed to this change were the growing emphasis on the worth and responsibility of the individual (which had its roots in pre-exilic prophetic preaching) and the shift of Israel's hope from the historical to the eschatological plane.

A growing individualization of the covenant is discernible in the period just prior to the exile. Thus while Jeremiah insisted that Israel was suffering for its national infidelity ("Your ways and your doings have brought this upon you. This is your doom, and it is bitter"[6]), the 'Book of Comfort' in the same tradition promised a new covenant, this time written on the heart, by which "all shall know [the Lord], from the least...to the greatest."[7] The growing individualization brought a new moral responsibility; under this covenant it shall no longer be said that

> "The fathers have eaten sour grapes,
> "and the children's teeth are set on edge."
> But every one shall die for his own sin;
> each man who eats sour grapes,
> his teeth shall be set on edge.[8]

There was, moreover, increasing testimony after the exile to the conviction that Sheol lay open before the Lord [9] (as evidenced in the miraculous powers of Elijah and Elisha[10]), that God's power extended to Sheol, although its exercise there was at first seen to be exceptional. Gradually it

[6]Jer 4:18.

[7]Jer 31:34.

[8]Jer 31:30; cf. Deut 24:16.

[9]Psalm 49:15; R.H. Charles, *Eschatology: the Doctrine of a Future Life in Israel, Judaism and Christianity — A Critical History* (New York: Schocken Books, 1963), 57, 75ff.

[10]2 Kings 2:11-12; 13:20-21.

came to be believed that the covenantal God would "ransom [the] soul from the power of Sheol,"[11] that there was hope of life after death and that one could say of God, as did the psalmist that

> Nevertheless I am continually with thee;
> thou dost hold my right hand.
> Thou dost guide me with thy counsel,
> and afterward thou wilt receive me to glory.[12]

In the early understanding of the covenant a misfortune of the magnitude of the exile would have been interpreted as a punishment for national disloyalty to Yahweh. However, resistance to the traditional answers and a questioning of divine power and justice is discernible behind the prophetic writings from the time immediately before the exile and after it. We read in Ezekiel:

> Yet the house of Israel says,
> "The way of the Lord is not just."[13]

And Jeremiah writes:

> And. . . you tell these people all these words, and they say to you, "Why has the Lord pronounced all this great evil against us? What is our iniquity? What is the sin that we have committed against the Lord our God?"[14]

It seems that the theology of history reflected in the books of Judges and Kings no longer commanded widespread assent, and that new explanations of misfortune had, therefore, to be sought.

One explanation, consistent with the growing stress on individual personal responsibility already mentioned, was

[11]Ps 49:15.
[12]Ps 73:23-24.
[13]Ezek 18:29.
[14]Jer 16:10.

to link personal suffering with individual sin. A theory of personal, rather than national, judgement, however, brought into sharp relief the problem of innocent suffering. If hope cannot be projected onto the future well-being of the nation, where does it lie? The corollary of the prophetic emphasis on the ethical responsibility of the individual had been the affirmation of the justice of God, yet there was little, if any, basis in the pre-exilic doctrine of Sheol for the reward of the just and the punishment of the wicked. The wisdom literature of the fourth and third centuries is individualistic, universalist (it has been called "an international quest for the meaning of life"[15]) and without illusions. The book of Job, for instance, is one long commentary on the divine injustice is so evident to the protagonist as he contemplates the destruction of his family and the finality of death.

> For there is hope for a tree,
> if it be cut down, that it will sprout again,
> and that its shoots will not cease....
> But man dies, and is laid low;
> man breathes his last, and where is he?
> As waters fail from a lake,
> and a river wastes away and dries up,
> so man lies down and rises not again;
> till the heavens are no more he will not awake
> or be roused out of his sleep.[16]

Job, unconvinced by the platitudes of Eliphaz, Zophar and Bildad, is voicing the challenge that human experience has always offered to the traditional notion that the just will be rewarded on earth.

> I have heard many such things;
> miserable comforters are you all....
> God gives me up to the ungodly,
> and casts me into the hands of the wicked.

[15]Joel Kuntz, *The People of Ancient Israel* (New York: Harper and Row, 1974).
[16]Job 14:7, 10-12.

I was at ease, and he broke me asunder;
he seized me by the neck and dashed me to pieces;
he set me up as his target,
his archers surround me....
My friends scorn me;
my eye pours out tears to God,
that the would maintain the right of a man with God,
like that of a man with his neighbour....
My spirit is broken, my days are extinct,
the grave is ready for me.[17]

Job, who "[has] uttered what [he] did not understand,"[18] could take refuge only in divine incomprehensibility, but, with the covenant individualized and the notion of divine faithfulness and justice deeply engrained, the hope of a retributive afterlife could not be long in entering jewish thought. Brandon writes: "The concept of a just and omnipotent God demanded an eschatology which promised that the justice of his dealing with individual men and women would be vindicated after death, since too often it was not demonstrated in this life."[19]

Not surprisingly, concurrent with the increasingly personal emphasis of the covental relationship there was a shift in Israel's hope from the historical to the eschatological plane. Historical misfortunes were now seen less as a punishment for faithlessness and more as a purifying preparation for vindication beyond history. While some (e.g. Ezekiel) expected the eschatological kingdom to be restricted to Israelites: others (e.g. Jeremiah) looked for its initiation in Israel, to be followed by openness to the just of all nations.

These hopes for an eschatological re-establishment of Israel were sometimes conveyed in images which indicate

17Job 16:2, 11-13a, 20-21; 17:1.
18Job 42:3b.
19Brandon, 63.

"the physical re-constitution of the dead."[20] Best known is Ezekiel's vision in the valley of bones.

> And [the Lord] said to me, "Son of man, can these bones live?" And I answered, "O Lord God, thou knowest." Again he said to me, "Prophesy to these bones and say to them, 'O dry bones, hear the word of the Lord. Thus says the Lord God to these bones: Behold, I will cause breath to enter you, and you shall live. And I will lay sinews upon you, and will cause flesh to come upon you, and cover you with skin, and put breath in you, and you shall live; and you shall know that I am the Lord.'"[21]

As Brandon says in the same discussion, "The physical re-constitution of the dead, and their re-animation, were demanded by the Hebrew conception of man [as psycho-physical organism] as the essential preconditions for such an act of vindication."[22]

It should be noted that the eschatological hopes of the individual and of the nation were not totally separate from each other; indeed, some commentators see a synthesis of the two occurring about 200 B.C.E. Charles stresses that the expectation was that "the righteous individual no less than the righteous nation [would] participate in the messianic kingdom, for the righteous dead of Israel will rise to share therein."[23] While Moore has called the notion of personal judgement "the ultimate step in the individualization of religion" and that of the messianic age "the ultimate nation-alization," he points out that both expectations co-existed in the hope of the resurrection of the righteous Israelite at

---

[20]Brandon, 64.

[21]Ezek 37:3-6.

[22]Brandon, 64.

[23] Charles, 130.

the beginning of the messianic age.[24] So closely are the ideas entwined that it is problematic whether some passages (e.g. Isaiah 25-26) refer to the giving of new life to the individual or to the nation. This alternative may indeed be a false one inasmuch as the Israelite was seen as rising to new life only as a member of the re-created nation, when its sins would be forgiven, its wrongs righted and its hopes fulfilled.

It is not unlikely that the zoroastrian beliefs in individual judgement and the resurrection of the body to a fresh beginning with God in heaven — beliefs about which the Jews would have heard both from Persians in Babylon and from travelers to Jerusalem — influenced their eschatology.[25] Despite the stirrings of national and individual eschatological hopes, the conclusions that there was a judgement and the possibility of a happy afterlife were not quickly or easily drawn. It was not in fact until the problem of the suffering of the just in its most acute form—martyrdom—served as the catalyst that belief in resurrection entered jewish thought in any significant way. The event which sparked the unequivocal articulation of belief in resurrection (or better, some would say, the re-creation) of the just among many, but not all Jews, was the rebellion of the Maccabees in 167 B.C.E. The hope of those martyred for fidelity of the Law ("we are ready to die rather than transgress the laws of our fathers"[26]) is expressed in the second of the books which bear their name (written in the second half of the second century B.C.E.) by one of the dying brothers:

> [Y]ou dismiss us from this present life, but the king
> of the universe will raise us up to an everlasting
> renewal of life, because we have died for his laws.[27]

---

[24]George Foot M. Moore, *Judaism in the First Centuries of the Christian Era* (Cambridge, Mass.: Harvard University Press, 1927), II, 377.

[25]R.C. Zaehner, *The Teachings of the Magi*, London: George Allen & Unwin. 1956, pp.131-150.

[26]2 Macc 7:2.

[27]2 Macc 7:9.

Another, offering his hands to the fire, says:

> I got these from Heaven, and because of his laws I
> disdain them, and from him I hope to get them back
> again.[28]

Finally their mother affirms her belief in the justice of the
Creator:

> [T]he Creator of the world, who shaped the beginning of
> man and devised the origin of all things, will in his
> mercy give life and breath back to you again, since
> you now forget yourselves for the sake of his laws [29]

It should be noted that in the maccabean eschatology it is
the just of Israel who are raised to life, for their persecutors
"there will be no resurrection to life."[30] But a contemporary
writer, also provoked by the heroic witness, spells out the
negative judgement:

> At that time. . . many of those who sleep in the dust of
> the earth shall awake, some to everlasting life, and
> some to shame and everlasting contempt. And those who
> are wise shall shine like the brightness of the firmament,
> and those who turn many to righteousness like the
> stars for ever and ever.[31]

The apocalyptic vision of Daniel (from which this last passage was taken) was not forgotten, but it was not developed
as much as it might have been. The ideas presented to the
jewish world from the fourth century B.C.E on by a greek
dualistic anthropology which taught the independent survival of the soul, happily released from the body, introduced a
competing understanding of the afterlife. Evidence can be

[28] 2 Macc 7:11.
[29] 2 Macc 7:23.
[30] 2 Macc 7:9, 14.
[31] Dan 12:2-3.

found, particularly in late Old Testament wisdom writings of ideas of an (at least temporary) survival of the soul independent of the body. Thus the Wisdom of Solomon asserts that

> ...the souls of the righteous are in the hand of God,
> and no torment will ever touch them.
> In the eyes of the foolish they seem to have died,
> and their departure was thought to be an affliction,
> and their going from us to be their destruction;
> but they are at peace.
> For though in the sight of men they were punished,
> their hope is full of immortality.[32]

The notion that the eternal life of the soul does not necessarily mean the resurrection of the body (although, of course, it need not preclude it) was both a contributing and a confusing factor in the growing jewish belief in a life after death. Doctrines of the immortality of the soul and of the resurrection of the body had, however, at least one element in common. Just as the jewish understanding of death differed from that of other ancient cultures in seeing it as the result of a direct intervention of God (the punishment for sin [Gen 3:19]), so the continuing life of the soul, as well as the resurrection of the body, is understood as God's direct gift, in no way belonging to it in virtue of its nature. It has been suggested that eventually the two notions—that of resurrection and that of the independent survival of the soul—were conflated by the introduction of the idea of an intermediate state between death and the eschatological denouement.[33]

The idea of an afterlife for the individual and, to a lesser extent, that of the resurrection of the just gained widespread, but not universal, acceptance in late second temple Judaism. They appear frequently in intertestamental literature (*Enoch, Jubilees, The Testament of the Twelve Patri-*

[32]Wis 3:1-4.

[33]Paul Hoffman, "Auferstehung der Toten: Neues Testament," *Theologische Realenzyklopadie* (1979), IV, 445.

archs) and the Pharisees established them as doctrines. The Sadducees, however, maintained the older tradition and rejected the possibility of resurrection, and so the notion had still to be defended and justified, as the following passage indicates:

> [Judas Maccabeus] took up a collection, man by man, to the amount of two thousand drachmas of silver, and sent it to Jerusalem to provide for a sin offering. In doing this he acted very well and honorably, taking account of the resurrection. For if he were not expecting that those who had fallen would rise again, it would have been superfluous and foolish to pray for the dead. But if he was looking to the splendid reward that is laid up for those who fall asleep in godliness, it was a holy and pious thought.[34]

It is against this wider jewish background that one can understand that primitive Christianity may have had the appearance, for a time at least, of "a resurrectionist sect within Judaism."[35] What is clear is that in the jewish development of the idea of bodily resurrection "a language had been forged" by means of which, as Dubarle points out, the christian hope would be expressed.[36]

The New Testament

While jewish views of life after death provided the remote background for the thought of the patristic age on death and resurrection, its immediate source was, of course, the apostolic tradition. The New Testament is totally informed by the resurrection of Jesus and the hope it engendered among his followers, and it also gives evidence of the developments in the early christian understanding of its significance.

---

[34]2 Macc 12:43-45.
[35]C.F. Evans, *Resurrection and the New Testament* (London: SCM, 1981), 20.
[36]Dubarle, 39.

Although the resurrection of the dead was a topic for discussion in first century Judaism, it is conspicuously infrequent, either as a theme or a problem, in the synoptic gospels, and Jesus appears to have had little to say about it. There is no mention of it, for example, in the markan apocalypse of chapter thirteen (the reason may be, of course, that the eschatological day of reckoning described there was expected within the lifetime of those to whom the gospel was directed). In general, the emphasis in Jesus' message as found in the synoptics is on the imminent presence of the Kingdom of God, rather than on the future hope,[37] and, as more than one scholar has pointed out, it is precisely that imminence which most distinguished Jesus' teaching from jewish apocalyptic pronouncements of the first century.[38] As confidence in that imminent eschatological breakthrough faded among Christians generally Paul's expectation of the resurrection of the dead was adopted as the unchallenged centre of their hope.

The only synoptic text discussing (rather than merely alluding to) the resurrection of the body is found in the exchange between Jesus and the Sadducees concerning the implication of levirate marriage for the afterlife (Mk 12:18ff and parallels). It is worth remarking that Jesus does not try to convince the Sadducees of the resurrection of the dead, but focuses instead on the power of God and the nature of the resurrection life. He points out that their derisory question is based on a materialist understanding of life after death as merely a continuation of that on earth. Jesus is recorded as telling the Sadducees that this assumption shows that they are ignorant of both "the scriptures [and] the power of God" (v.24), and that they are blind to the divine power which will transform human life into a form resembling that of the angels (v.25b). The implication of these reproofs is that the Sadducees are so bound, even in their imaginations, to the material world that they cannot

---

[37]Hoffman, 450; cf. Evans, 31-33.

[38]Hoffman, 451; G. Rochais, *Les recits de resurrection des morts dans le nouveau Testament* (Cambridge: Cambridge University Press, 1981), 185.

envisage an afterlife in which the body will be spiritual.

Jesus then goes on to remind the Sadducees that Moses referred to God as "the God of Abraham and ...of Isaac...and of Jacob"—all dead long before. The inference is either that their souls live on or, more probably, that their relationship with God will be re-established when they are raised from Sheol.[39] The latter would be in keeping with the fact that Jesus' few references to resurrection are usually in the context of those from past generations—the men of Nineveh, the Queen of the South[40]—who will be raised for judgement (a judgement expected within the generation of those who heard him), rather than of promises for the future.[41]

When we widen our examination of the New Testament beyond texts dealing explicitly with the resurrection of the dead we note, however, a characteristic thrust towards the future in many of the parables and sayings attributed to Jesus. The preaching of the coming of the Kingdom of God, imminent or remote, is not, of course, simply convertible with an expectation of resurrection, but, in the context of late jewish eschatological hopes, it is not implausible to give it that colouration. Furthermore, many passages in the New Testament attribute sayings to Jesus apparently predicated on "a certain definition of human life which...is...highly congruous with [resurrection], once that came to be stated."[42] Included here are all those sayings which tie together behaviour in this life and the quality of the life to come, i.e. those dealing with or implying judgement, such as this from Luke's gospel:

> [W]hen you give a feast, invite the poor, the maimed, the lame, the blind, and you will be blessed, because they

[39]E.E. Ellis, "Jesus, the Sadducees and Qumran," *NTS* 10 (1963-64), 275.

[40]Mt 12:41, 42.

[41]Richard H. Hiers, *The Historical Jesus and the Kingdom of God* (Gainesville, Florida: University of Florida Press, 1973), 27.

[42]Evans, 36.

cannot repay you. You will be repaid at the resurrection
of the just.[43]

The difficulty of discerning the nature of Jesus' eschatological expectations for himself and his followers lies, of
course, in the lack of agreement concerning the extent to
which the New Testament depiction of him was informed by
the understanding of the post-resurrection christian community. (The resurrection experience of the first Christians
has been memorably compared [in an algebraic metaphor]
to the transcendental 'sign' outside the historical 'bracket,'
the sign which determines the evaluation of all the events
within the bracket.[44]) In the light of this experience, Jesus'
words and actions were inevitably remembered as at least
open to, if not expecting, his continued existence and future
vindication.[45] The ministry and preaching of Jesus can,
however, be said to have been readily intelligible in the
context of an anticipation of resurrection, or as a life and
actions characterized by a capacity or even a 'crying-out' for
resurrection as a consequence, not a reward.[46] It has also
been said that Jesus' actions prophetically proclaimed and
inaugurated the Kingdom of God which, "according to the
apocalyptic understanding of the age," would come only
after the general resurrection, the coming of the Son of man
and the judgement.[47]

We know of the resurrection experience of the early
Christian community directly through the accounts in the
New Testament of its encounters with the risen Christ and
indirectly through the ambience and hope in which the first
Christians lived. The direct witness, because it attempts to
relate the transcendent in terms of historical narrative (the
stories of the resurrection appearances), is in some ways less
informative than the indirect (the inferences that can be

[43]Lk 14:13-14; cf. 16:19ff.
[44]Evans, 62.
[45]Evans, 39.
[46]Evans, 36.
[47]Rochais, 185.

drawn from our knowledge of the primitive church). While the various New Testament accounts of the resurrection appearances reflect different experiences and have different particular points to make, in all there is indication of a recognition of Jesus' life renewed; and their combined proclamation is "the exaltation of Jesus to universal status and authority, the effusion of the Spirit, the apostolic mission of the church to the world, and the understanding of the gospel in the light of [Old Testament] scripture."[48] Some accounts portray Jesus as raised with a revivified body which lacks only the spatial and temporal limitations of his historical body, while others, in which he is not recognized by his disciples until his actions reveal his identity, give a significantly different impression.[49] It has been suggested that the accounts which present Jesus' resurrection in terms of an explicitly material body are voicing, in the light of traditional jewish anthropology in which bodily life is the proper mode of human existence, "an unqualified identification of the risen Christ with the earthly Jesus."[50] Similarly, another writer sees reflected in these accounts the conviction that Jesus' resurrection life has caught up his historical life without destroying it, that "it was not only Jesus who rose, but his whole life ith him."[51] Evans writes that "Resurrection. . . as the more concrete and cruder term [compared with the johannine 'exaltation'] directs attention not only forward but also backwards. As reversal and resuscitation it is the recovery intact from death of this particular man, and of what made him the particular man he was.... The historical past is not discarded as a snake sloughs off its skin, but is recovered."[52]

If this view is correct, then, whenever the materiality of Jesus' resurrection body is stressed in the New Testament

[48]C.F. Evans, 132.
[49]Cf. e.g. Lk 24:36ff and 24:16ff.
[50]Neville Clark, *Interpreting the Resurrection* (London: SCM, 1967), 85.
[51]Scott Holland cited in Evans, 142.
[52]Evans, 142.

accounts, our attention is being directed backward in order to teach the ongoing living integrity of his person, i.e. he who lives again is the same person as the disciples knew in Palestine and Jerusalem. Similarly, its forward thrust may be said to be an affirmation of the continuing incarnation of God, although in a different modality.

Jesus' resurrection was understood first as a vindication, a promise of the imminent Kingdom of God, and was therefore seen in the light of the parousia, as the necessary prelude to his second coming. As long as the parousia was the focus of hope, the salvation of Christians depended on their being present with him then. Thus Paul praises the thessalonian Christians for waiting "for [God's] Son from heaven, whom he raised from the dead, Jesus who delivers us from the wrath to come."[53] But, as the hope of the parousia became more and more remote, the resurrection of Jesus replaced his second coming as the focus of faith. As a corollary, the resurrection of Christians (which had begun on the parousial axis as well, as an assurance that their deaths before Jesus' second coming would not put them beyond the reach of his saving power) was more urgently and yet more remotely the focus of hope.

It is in Paul's letters that we have not only the earliest resurrection account (1 Cor 15:3-8), but also the earliest evaluation of Jesus' cross and resurrection as redemptive, overcoming both sin and death. Because in the judaeo-christian understanding the two are seen as having entered the world together as a consequence of Adam's fall, they must be overcome together, and hence Paul's christological title for the risen Jesus of 'last Adam,' the head and representative of the new age.

Stanley has traced in detail the evolution of Paul's understanding of the resurrection of Jesus and of the Christian; only a few of the most important stages can be outlined here.[54] He points out that Paul early in his career "asserts a

[53] 1 Thess 1:9-10.

[54] D. Stanley, *Christ's Resurrection in Pauline Soteriology* (Rome: Pont. Bib. Inst., 1961).

causal connection between Christ's resurrection and that of
the Christian ('For since we believe that Jesus died and rose
again, even so, through Jesus, God will bring with him those
who have fallen asleep,' 1 Thess 4:14ff), but the connecting
link does not appear as anything intrinsic to the risen Christ.
It is rather the infallible will of God."[55] In Phil 3:9-11,
however, it is the righteousness of faith which, in transform-
ing knowledge, unites the Christian to the risen Christ as a
preparation for resurrection ("[that I may have] the righteousness from God which depends on faith; that I may
know him and the power of his resurrection, and may share
his sufferings, becoming like him in his death, that if possible I may attain the resurrection from the dead").[56] Stanley
points out that in verses 20-21 of the same chapter ("from
[heaven] we await a Saviour, the Lord Jesus Christ, who will
change our lowly body to be like his glorious body, by the
power which enables him even to subject all things to himself") there is "one of the very rare places...where the
power which effects the resurrection of the just is attributed,
not to the Father, but to Christ."[57]

Yet, while faith in the resurrection of Jesus was shared by
all who called themselves Christians (Paul appeals to it in 1
Cor 15:12-19 as the common premise on which he and the
Corinthians agree), it is evident that the futurity of the
resurrection of Christians was a matter of some debate.
Evans suggests that the Corinthians' position may have
been the same as that of Hymenaeus and Philetus, who
"have swerved from the truth by holding that [the resurrec-
tion] is past already" (2 Tim 2:18).[58] (This belief of some
Christians that there was no future resurrection may have
stemmed from Paul's proleptic anticipation of the Kingdom; we meet the same anticipation in the fourth gospel.) In
1 Cor 15:12-13, 17-18, the classic resurrection passage

[55]Stanley, 88.
[56]Stanley, 102-105.
[57]Stanley, 107; cf. 1 Cor 6:14.
[58]Evans, 156-157.

("Now if Christ is preached as raised from the dead, how can
some of you say that there is no resurrection of the dead?
But if there is no resurrection of the dead, then Christ has
not been raised. . . . If Christ has not been raised, your faith
is futile and you are still in you sins. Then those also who
have fallen asleep in Christ have perished."). "Paul proves
the fact of the general resurrection from the truth of Christ's
resurrection,"[59] and derives his understanding of the mode
of the resurrection bodies of the just from that of Christ
("sown in dishonour, raised in glory, sown in weakness,
raised in strength, sown a physical body, raised a spiritual
body" (1 Cor 15:43-44). And finally, Stanley points out, in
Romans 4:25, the resurrection plays the same causal role in
relation to human justification as Jesus' death does to forgiveness; the Christian has been made 'alive to God' spiritually and, in hope, bodily.[60]

The resurrectional and eschatological teaching of the
fourth gospel is less clear, less straightforward than Paul's—
almost all contemporary scholarship on the gospel talks of
'tension' in its teaching on these subjects. 'Ascent' and 'exaltation,' rather than 'resurrection' are the theological cur-
rency of this gospel; the evangelist plays with the concept of
'being lifted up' and uses it in a double sense: physically on
the cross (which is the beginning of Jesus' glorification) and
spiritually, "a removal into the divine sphere and life."[61]
There is, therefore, a perception that neither the resurrection stories surrounding Jesus nor the expectation of bodily
resurrection for Christians fit in exactly with the tone of the
rest of the gospel. Evans writes that "strictly speaking, there
is no place in the Fourth Gospel for resurrection stories,
since the ascent or exaltation has already taken place.
Nevertheless, and doubtless in deference to Christian tradition, the evangelist supplies three. . . ."[62]

[59]Stanley, 118 (emphasis his); for a contrary view, cf. Clark, 51.

[60]Stanley, 173.

[61]Evans, 139; cf. 116.

[62]Evans, 116.

If this assessment is accurate, these three stories speak volumes about the ambivalence in the belief of the church at the end of the first century concerning the resurrection body of Jesus. Even someone as committed to a 'spiritual' understanding of the christian message as the fourth evangelist was constrained to include one story of resurrection appearances—the overcoming of Thomas' doubts, 20:26-29—which implies a physical body. But, equally noteworthy, two of the other stories—that of Mary Magdalen, who does not at first recognize her Lord and is forbidden to touch him (20:11-18), and that of Jesus appearing among his disciples through closed doors (20:19)—imply precisely the opposite. The question of the nature of Jesus' risen body (and therefore of the future resurrection body of the Christian) was still apparently an open one, but it was not to be seen to be so for long. Grant writes (in perhaps somewhat of an overstatement) that, "The Fourth Evangelist is the last Christian writer considered orthodox by the ancient church who stresses the spiritual nature of the risen body of Christ."[63] It is the case that in the second century new polemical concerns would lead to a shift in emphasis in the teaching about the risen Jesus and the hoped-for resurrection of Christians.

Allusion has already been made to the tension between present and future eschatology which is found throughout the New Testament: the Kingdom of God is future, but in some manner already present in Jesus' ministry; God's action in raising Jesus to be already the Christ (i.e. not waiting for the parousia) is recognized as belonging to the eschaton, 'tomorrow' is seen to be 'now.' "The last Day at the end of history had taken shape on the third day in the midst of history."[64] Nowhere is this paradox and tension clearer than in the fourth gospel where it is manifested in the double emphasis on the present realization of eternal life

[63]R.M. Grant, "The Resurrection of the Body," *Journal of Religion* 27 (1948), 120-130, 188-208.

[64]Clark, 52.

(the 'vertical' understanding) and on the future resurrection of the Christian (the 'horizontal' understanding). Brown suggests that what is reflected here is not the pressure of the belief of the community upon the evangelist (as some have thought), but a tension in Jesus' teaching itself between the present possibility of eternal life (echoed in the christian community's conviction that Jesus had "introduced a definitive moment in human existence"[65]) and "the future vision of glory when [the Christian] joins Jesus in the Father's presence."[66] While there are clear allusions to resurrection and judgement in the fourth gospel (5:28-29; 6:39-40; 6:44,54; 12:48), it may be that one of the reasons for the emphasis on the present possibility of eternal life was the evangelist's perception of the need to overcome the disappoinment and scepticism resulting from the destruction of the Temple in 70 C.E.—the removal of the "last tangible sign" of the imminent parousia.[67] There are doublets in the gospel, presenting the same teaching in apocalyptic and realized eschatological terms (e.g. 5:19-25 and 26-29), and Brown concludes that, "[W]e may expect to find in John traces of the swinging to and fro of eschatological expectation in the first century."[68]

The legacy of the New Testament to the patristic age on the subject of death was clear: death, both physical and spiritual, was a result of Adam's sin, but that double death had been overcome, new life given in the death and resurrection of Jesus. God had raised Jesus—on that all Christians were agreed—and Paul's term 'firstfruits' probably accurately reflected their understanding of Christ not only as the temporal first, but as the representative, "the first-born among many brethren" (Rom 8:25).[69] And, although the

---

[65]R.E. Brown, *The Gospel according to John* (Garden City, N.Y.: Doubleday, 1966), I,cxvii.

[66]Brown, cxviii.

[67]Brown, cxx.

[68]Brown, cxx.

[69]Clark, 60.

resurrection of the Christian to judgement had become a 'doctrinal commonplace' by the end of the New Testament period ("Therefore let us leave the elementary doctrines of Christ and go on to maturity, not laying again a foundation of repentance from dead works and of faith toward God, with instruction about ablutions, the laying on of hands, the resurrection of the dead, and eternal judgement"),[70] the teaching of the christian community on bodily resurrection remained ambiguous. Christ shared his eschatological victory with his disciples, they had been "born anew to a living hope through the resurrection of Jesus Christ from the dead" (1 Pet 1:3). But the degree and manner of that present sharing, the balance between realization and hope and the nature of that future life with Christ and the Father was variously understood and open to speculation.

[70]Heb 6:1-2; cf. Hoffman, 462.

2. THE APOSTOLIC FATHERS

The writings of those known collectively as the 'Apostolic Fathers' date from the late first and early second centuries of the christian era. In them, human death is commonly accepted as the result of sin,[1] and the salvific significance of Christ's death is variously presented. There is still evidence of interest in the parousia, but the resurrection of Christ and of Christians is treated in a surprisingly peripheral way. Resurrection is not in itself often a focus of discussion and, where it does occur, it is subordinated to other concerns: exhortations to the christian life, rejection of a docetic christology or expectation of the millenial reign of Christ. Although the risen Christ is mentioned several times as first fruits,[2] and as warrant for the mission and credibility of the church,[3] the characteristically pauline causal link between his resurrection and that hoped for by his followers receives relatively little attention.

There was apparently difference of opinion among the Apostolic Fathers on the scope of the resurrection: will all the raised to be judged (Polycarp, *2 Clement*, Barnabas), or will the judgment precede the resurrection and only the just

[1]Cf. e.g. *Barn.* 12.5b/
[2]E.g. *I Clem.* 24.1.
[3]E.g. *I Clem.* 42.1-3.

be raised (the author of the *Didache*, Papias, Ignatius)? There is also a lack of clarity concerning the meaning these writers gave to 'body' and consequently concerning the nature of the resurrection body: did they mean the material element in contrast to the spiritual, or the "organic principle of self-identity,"[4] or was it for them the symbol of "fully personal life?"[5] The question was not raised explicitly as a matter of controversy, as it would be in later centuries, and so their positions have frequently to be inferred. It can be seen, however, that in general the Apostolic Fathers were moving towards a more material understanding of the resurrection than that held by Paul and John.[6]

Many reasons have been advanced to account for this trend. The struggle against a docetic christology may have led to a selective emphasis on those aspects in the stories of the appearances of the risen Christ which stressed his material body (his eating with the disciples, Lk 24:14; Thomas Didymus being invited to touch his wounds, Jn 20:27), and these accounts may then have been taken as criteria for the resurrection hoped for by Christians.[7] This expectation was in marked and already conscious contrast to the soteriology of some types of Gnosticism, i.e. the salvation through esoteric knowledge through the soul alone (although it is said that at least one early gnostic leader, Menander, also promised resurrection of the body).[8] Christianity as well both inherited many of the hopes of jewish apocalyptic, with its vivid depictions of the reward of the just in a new material creation, and saw the need to provide an alternative to these visions in the idea (held by some, but not all) of a millenarian rule of Christ to be shared by the just, their bodies

---

[4]R.M. Grant, "The Resurrection of the Body," *Journal of Religion* 27 (1948), 124, quoting C.H. Dodd.

[5]J.G. Davies, "Factors leading to the Emergence of Belief in the Resurrection of the Flesh," *Journal of Theological Studies* 23 (1972), 448-55.

[6]Cf. especially Davies, Grant and A. O'Hagan, *Material Re-creation in the Apostolic Fathers* (Berlin: Akademie-Verlag, 1968).

[7]Davies, 448.

[8]Cf. Irenaeus, *Adversus Haereses* I.24.2.

physically renewed.[9] Finally, an interesting connection has recently been suggested between interpretations of certain christian teachings relating to the body (incarnation, resurrection, asceticism) and concomitant attitudes to the church and secular society.[10]

As the writings of the individual Apostolic Fathers are examined, it will be seen that their various treatments of the resurrection of Christians can be best understood by an examination of the context of each work. For some the resurrection was brought to the service of exhortation of virtue (*1 Clement, 2 Clement*, the *Didache*), for others to that of christology (Ignatius' letters), and there are those for whom it seems to have been a necessary component of a general material re-creation (the *Letter of Barnabas*, the fragments of Papias).

First Clement, Second Clement, The Didache

The context of *1 Clement* was one of remonstration with the faction-ridden church at Corinth, and the hope of the resurrection of the Christians was fitted into the exhortations directed to that church. Christologically, the focus of the letter is less on Christ's death and resurrection than on his salvific revelatory function.

> This is the way, beloved, in which we found our salvation, Jesus Christ, the high priest of our offerings, the protector and helper of our weakness.
> Through him we fix our eyes on the heights of heaven,
> Through him we see mirrored the flawless and sublime countenance of God,
> Through him the eyes of our heart have been opened,

---

[9]Cf. e.g. Davies and O'Hagan.

[10]J. Gager, "Body Symbols and Social Reality: Resurrection, Incarnation and Asceticism in Early Christianity," *Religion* 12 (1982), 347, quoting Mary Douglas: "Doctrines which use the human body as their metaphor...are likely to be especially concerned with social relationships."

Through him our foolish and darkened understanding
springs up to the light,
Through him the Master has willed that we should taste
immortal knowledge.[11]

The 'immortal knowledge' brought by Christ finds expression in the apostolic teaching, and the resurrection is
brought forward as a guarantee of the validity of that
teaching.

The apostles received the gospel for us from Jesus Christ,
and Jesus the Christ was sent from God. So Christ is from
God and the apostles are from Christ: thus both came in
proper order by the will of God. And so the apostles, after
they had received their orders and in full assurance by
reason of the resurrection of our Lord Jesus Christ, being
full of faith in the word of God, went out in the conviction
of the Holy Spirit preaching the good news that God's
kingdom was about to come.[12]

In the context of the quarrels in the church of Corinth,
God's patient providence directed to peace and harmony
was held up as an ideal,[13] and God's faithfulness as the
answer to the 'double-minded' whose loss of hope in the
parousia was given as an excuse for their behavior:

The all-merciful and beneficent Father has mercy upon
those who fear him, and kindly and lovingly bestows his
favor upon those who approach him in singleness of
mind. Wherefore let us not be double-minded, neither let
our souls entertain false ideas about his surpassing and
glorious gifts. Far be that Scripture from us which says,

---

[11]*Clem.* 36.1-2. All quotations from *1 Clement* and *2 Clement* are taken from
R.M. Grant and H.H. Graham, *The Apostolic Fathers: a New Translation and
Commentary*, vol. 2 (New York: Thomas Nelson and Sons, 1965).

[12]*1 Clem.* 42.1-3.

[13]*1 Clem.* 19.2-3.

"Wretched are the double-minded, those who harbor
doubts in their souls and say, 'We have heard those things
even in our fathers' time, and yet here we are, already
grown old, and none of these things has happened to us.'
O senseless ones! Compare yourselves to a tree. Take a
vine, for instance: first it sheds its leaves, then comes a
bud, then a leaf, then a flower, and only after this, first a
green grape and then a ripe one." You see how in a short
space of time the fruit of the tree reaches maturity. Truly
his purpose will be quickly and suddenly accomplished,
just as the Scripture confirms when it says, "He will come
quickly and not delay, and the Lord will come suddenly
to his temple, even the Holy one whom you expect."[14]

This coming of the Holy One will include the resurrection
"of which [God] made our Lord Jesus Christ the first fruits
when he raised him from the dead."[15] It has been persua-
sively argued that the theological underpinning of *1 Clement* is a very positive understanding of creation and of the
reliability of divine providence.[16] Consistent with this analysis, it is interesting to note that, although referring to Christ
as "first fruits," the letter does not link the resurrection of
the Christian directly with that of Christ, but instead makes
great use of analogies from nature in arguing for the resurrection of the just. The signs from nature include not only
the metaphor of the vine just quoted, but the inference of
divine faithfulness that the author believed could reliably be
drawn from the regularity and dependability of the diurnal
and seasonal cycles.

Let us consider, beloved, how the Master continually
points out that future resurrection which is to be, of

[14] *1 Clem.* 23.1-5.

[15] *1 Clem.* 24.1.

[16] T.H.C. van Eijk, *La resurrection des morts dans les Peres apostoliques* (Paris:
Beauchesne, 1974), 44ff. Although my brief summary of the Apostolic Fathers'
treatment of the resurrection cannot take into account much of van Eijk's careful
analysis, I am greatly indebted to this, the definitive work on the subject to date.

which he made our Lord Jesus Christ the first fruits when he raised him from the dead. Let us observe, beloved, the resurrection that occurs in the regularity of the seasons. Day and night manifest resurrection: night falls asleep, and day arises; day departs, night returns. Or take for example the crops: how and in what way is the sowing done? The sower goes out and sows each seed in the ground, and they fall in the earth dry and bare, and decay. Then from their decay the wondrous providence of the Master raises them, and from each one more grow and bear fruit.[17]

An even more vivid assurance is found in the legend of the phoenix, the bird said to rise from its own ashes.

Are we to think it then a great and wondrous thing if the Creator of all things causes to be raised from the dead those who have served him in holiness and in the assurance of a good faith, when even in the case of a bird he shows us the greatness of his promise? For it says somewhere, "And thou shalt raise me up and I shall praise thee," and 'I lay down and slept: I rose up again, because thou art with me.' And again Job says, "And thou shalt raise up this flesh of mine which has endured all these things."[18]

God is here presented as raising only the just, and these passages on the resurrection are hardly more than supporting asides to the general parenetic intent of the letter.

How blessed and wonderful are the gifts of God, beloved! Life in immortality, splendor in righteousness, truth in boldness, faith in confidence, self-control in holiness; and all these fall within our comprehension. What things, then, are being prepared for those who wait for him? The

[17] *1 Clem.* 24.1-5.
[18] *1 Clem.* 26.1-2.

> Creator and Father of the ages, the all holy One himself
> knows their greatness and beauty. Let us therefore strive
> to be in the number of those that wait for him, so that we
> may share in the promised gifts.[19]

Because discussion of resurrection is so subordinated to the
letters' general thrust it is difficult to determine the author's
understanding of the character of the resurrection body.
The frequent comparisons with the natural world might
suggest that he had a revivified material body in mind, but it
is equally likely that he found them simply convenient analogies. It is interesting to note that the letter contains one of
the two passages in the Apostolic Fathers which seems to
affirm the survival of the soul independently of the body.

> All the generations from Adam to our day have passed
> away, but those made perfect in love according to the
> grace of God have a place among the godly who will be
> made manifest when Christ's kingdom comes. For it is
> written, "Enter into your inner rooms for a little while,
> until my wrath and anger pass, and I will remember a
> good day and I will raise you up from you graves."[20]

It is evident, however, that the question is not an issue with
the author and that the passage is more likely than not an
unreflecting way of asserting the salvation of the just of the
Old Testament.

The so-called *Second Letter of Clement* (really a homily)
also treats the resurrection in the context of parenesis, but
with a different emphasis. Although the author echoes the
theme of *1 Clement* that the parousia and the resurrection
will come as the result of God's faithfulness (using the same
simile of the bare vine which will bear fruit again[21]), he rests
his argument on both the necessity of a resurrection in the

[19] *1 Clem.* 35.1-4.
[20] *1 Clem.* 50.3-4.
[21] *2 Clem.* 11.3.

flesh, if the rewards and punishments of the final judgement are to consistent with human earthly life, and on the fleshly character of christian salvation.

The homily opens with a strenuous reminder of the work of Christ—" how much suffering Jesus Christ endured for us,"[22] "he has given us light,"[23] "rescued us when we were perishing[24] —and of him as "the Judge of the living and the dead."[25] The appropriate response of the Christian— acknowledgement of Christ in word and deed—will be rewarded, according to Christ's promise, by "rest in the kingdom to come and in life eternal."[26] Repudiating those who, by denying the resurrection and the judgement of the flesh, might undercut its appeal for repentance, the homily urges that we "repent with all our hearts of the evil we have done in the flesh,"[27] and warns

> Further, let none of you say that this flesh is not judged nor does it rise again. Consider: in what state were you saved, in what state did you regain your sight, if it was not in this flesh? Hence it is necessary to guard the flesh as the temple of God. For as in the flesh you were called, in the flesh you will come. If Christ the Lord who saved us was first spirit but became flesh and in that state called us, so we also shall receive our reward in this flesh.[28]

The argument here is twofold: Christians receive salvation themselves in the flesh, and Christ, the means of salvation, was himself enfleshed. It is therefore appropriate that the future reward should also be "in the flesh." The eternal

[22] *2 Clem.* 1.2.
[23] *2 Clem* 1.4.
[24] *2 Clem.* 1.4.
[25] *2 Clem.* 1.1.
[26] *2 Clem.* 5.5.
[27] *2 Clem.8.2*; cf. 6.4-5, 7.
[28] *2 Clem.* 9.1-5.

punishment is understood in this homily to be material as well.

> [T]hose who have gone astray or denied Jesus either in word or in deed [will be] punished in dreadful torments and fire unquenchable.[29]

Resurrection of the body, in the understanding of *2 Clement*, is therefore not reserved to the just. But the essential reward of the just will be also to share in the Spirit, that is in the existence of Christ before the incarnation,[30] and existence shared by "the first Church, the spiritual one, which was created before the sun and the moon."[31]

The christological argument, it will have been observed, is pursued in the homily not in terms of a causal nexus between the resurrection of Christ and that of the Christian, but with reference to the incarnation. Linked with this conviction is an understanding of the church, the body of Christ, as spiritually pre-existent (with Christ) and with the capacity of returning to that existence.

> Now the Church, being spiritual, was made manifest in the flesh of Christ to show us that if any of us guard her in the flesh and it be not corrupted, he will receive her back in the Holy Spirit.[32]

Because the flesh is the 'copy' of the Spirit[33] it can be saved.

> No one who corrupts the copy will receive the original in its place. This, then, is what it means, brethren: guard the flesh that you may share in the Spirit.... This flesh is able to receive so great a life and immortality because the

[29]*2 Clem.* 17.7.
[30]*2 Clem.* 14.1-3.
[31]*2 Clem.* 14.1-3.
[32]*2 Clem.* 14.3.
[33]*2 Clem.* 14.3

Holy Spirit is closely joined to it, nor can anyone express or declare 'what things the Lord has prepared' for his elect.[34]

But equally, the homily warns, it can be condemned.

If we say that the flesh is the Church and the Spirit is Christ, then he who does violence to the Church does violence to Christ. Such a man will not share in the Spirit, which is the Christ.[35]

Against the background of this hope and this warning, the homily returns to the call for repentance and the reminder of the judgement:

Let us then do what is right, that we may finally be saved. Blessed are they who obey these injunctions; and, if for a little while they suffer in this world, they will gather the immortal harvest of the resurrection. So let not the pious man be grieved if at the present time he is miserable. A time of blessedness awaits him. When he has come to life again with the fathers above, he will rejoice in an eternity that knows no grief.[36]

The *Didache* is an anonymous treatise devoted to teaching the "two ways, the one of light, the other of darkness." To those in the way of light is given "knowledge and faith and immortality," made known already through "Jesus, your Servant,"[37] but the only reference to the future resurrection of the Christian comes in the last chapter, an apocalypse resembling that of Mark 13.

---

[34] *2 Clem.* 14.3,5.

[35] *2 Clem.* 14.4.

[36] *2 Clem.* 17.1-4.

[37] *Did.* 10.2. All quotations from the *Didache* and the *Letter of Barnabas* are taken from R.A. Kraft, *The Apostolic Fathers: a New Translation and Commentary*, vol. 3 (New York: Thomas Nelson and Sons, 1965).

> And then the signs of the truth will appear: first the sign spread out in heaven, then the sign of a sound of a trumpet, and thirdly, the resurrection of the dead, yet not of all (the dead), but as it was said: 'The Lord will come and all his saints with him.' Then the world will see the Lord coming on the clouds of heaven with power and dominion to repay each man according to his work, with justice, before all men and angels.[38]

The context and the message is the behavior appropriate for those who wait for Christ's coming and the reward for which they may hope.

Ignatius and Polycarp

Perhaps it was the urgency of the problems he was actually facing—heresy, church order, above all, the prospect of martyrdom—which kept the focus of Ignatius' writings away from eschatology. Or it may have been the conviction, more strongly expressed than by the other Apostolic Fathers, that, as he wrote to the Ephesians, "the last times" had already in some sense arrived.

> Thus all magic was dissolved and every bond of wickedness vanished; ignorance was abolished and the old kingdom was destroyed, since God was becoming manifest in human form for the newness of eternal life; what had been prepared by God had its beginning. Hence everything was shaken together, for the abolition of death was being planned.[39]

The emphasis in this passage is on the new age, but it is evident that Ignatius was more explicit than either of the two writers of the sub-apostolic age already examined in

[38] *Did.* 16.6-8.
[39] *Eph.* 19.3.

describing the death and resurrection of Christ as its effective beginning. Their salvific value is clearly expressed in the most detailed of three rules of faith contained in these letters. Ignatius insisted to the Smyrnaeans that

> [Christ] is truly of the family of David as to the flesh,
> Son of God by God's will and power,
> truly born of a virgin,
> baptized by John so that 'all righteousness' might be
> 'fullfilled' by him,
> truly nailed for us in the flesh
> under Pontius Pilate and the tetrarch Herod...
> so that he might set up an ensign forever
> through the resurrection
> for his saints and faithful....
> in the one body of his Church.[40]

In his use of 'ensign' [*susemon*] Ignatius had in mind Isaiah 5.26— [The Lord] will raise a signal for a nation afar off"—, that is, he was envisioning the standard that is both an identification of the leader and the focus of loyalty to which adherents flock and under which they serve and are rewarded.

This same interweaving of Christ's resurrection, the Christian's response to it and the resurrection of the Christian is presented in the letter to the Trallians.

> He was also truly raised from the dead, when his Father raised him up, as in similar fashion his Father will raise up in Christ Jesus us who believe him—without whom we have no true life.[41]

'The true life' that Christians have is the expression of 'the last times' already present, the raising-up remains in the future. But Ignatius' writings bear witness to how inextrica-

[40]*Smyrn.* 1.
[41]*Trall.* 9.2, cf. *Smyrn.* 1.2-2.1.

bly tied both are in his mind to Christ's death and resurrection: "the Lord's [day]—on which also our life arose through him and his death,"[42] "the church...at Philadelphia...[which is] fully assured of all mercy by his resurrection."[43]

There is some indication in Ignatius' letters of his vision of the future life. It would, for one thing, be that of a community. The vividness of that hope is evident in his description of the reunion of Christians at the resurrection: he aspires to be found to be Polycarp's disciple then, [44] and he asks for prayers: "May I rise again in [my bonds]...so that I may be found in the lot apportioned to the Ephesian Christians."[45] Ignatius frequently stressed the 'fleshy' character of Christ's resurrection. Some see this chiefly as his way of affirming the reality of salvation in Christ,[46] while others say that it marks a relaxing of the tension between flesh and spirit.[47] It is evident that much of Ignatius' writing about the resurrection of Christ was coloured by the context of his struggle against the docetists. One passage in particular has prompted the remark that Ignatius abandoned "all the tension and restraint inherent in the pauline and johannine accounts of Jesus' risen body, and opted for a lucan description as the most sutiable for his controverisal purpose."[48]
He wrote to the Smyrnaeans:

> For I know and am confident that even after the resurrection he was in the flesh. And when he came to those with Peter he said to them, 'Take, handle me, and see that I am not an incorporeal demon.' And they immediately

---

[42] *Mag.* 9.1.

[43] *Phil.* salutation.

[44] *Pol* 7.1.

[45] *Eph.* 11.2.

[46] Eijk, 129.

[47] R.M. Grant, *Miracle and Natural Law*. Amsterdam: North Holland and Publishing Company, 1952, 230.

[48] Grant, *J Rel.*, 127.

touched him and believed, being mingled with his flesh and spirit. Therefore they despised death and were found to be above death. And after the resurrection he ate and drank with them as a being of flesh, though he was spiritually united with the Father.[49]

And at the end of the same letter Ignatius saluted the church "in the name of Jesus Christ and in his flesh and blood, his passion and resurrection both fleshy and spiritual."[50] The probability that Ignatius' use of 'flesh' in these passages reflected a materialistic understanding of the risen body is heightened by his indication on six occasions that both 'body' and 'spirit' are necessary for the complete human person.[51]

And finally, there is also in Ignatius an interesting identification of the Eucharist with "the flesh of our Savior Jesus Christ which suffered for our sins, which the Father raised up by his goodness."[52] Partaking of the Eucharist is therefore spiritually therapeutic: "it is the medicine of immortality, the antidote which results not in dying but in living forever in Jesus Christ."[53] (This is the first post-scriptural appearance of a theme that would recur often in the patristic era.)

Like *1 Clement* and *2 Clement*, the letter of Polycarp to the Philippians is chiefly concerned with urging and encouraging them in the christian life. Polycarp, however, also dealt with two issues which touch directly on the resurrection, two issues which, because of the frequency of their appearance, we may assume were dividing the christian community at the time: loss of hope in the coming of the parousia, and denial of the reality both of Christ's body and of his death and of the resurrection and judgement of Chris-

---

[49]*Smyrn.* 3.1-3.

[50]*Smyrn.* 12.2.

[51]*Eph.* 7.2, *Mag.* 13.3, *Trall.* Salutation, *Smyrn.* 12.2, *Pol.* 1.2, 2.2.

[52]*Smyrn.* 7.1.

[53]*Eph.* 20.2.

tians. In response to the first—despair of the parousia—Polycarp presented the customary exhortation that God is worthy of belief in a passage that is a catena of New Testament phrases.

> Serve God in fear and truth; give up empty vain discussion and the error of the crowd; believe "him who raised our Lord Jesus Christ from the dead and gave him glory" and a throne at his right hand, to whom were subjected all things in heaven and earth, whom every breathing thing serves, who is coming as judge of the living and the dead, whose blood God will require of those who disobey him. And "he who raised him" from the dead "will also raise us" if we do his will and walk in his commandments. . . . [54]

And his warning to the nay-sayers was as strong as language will allow.

> For "everyone who does not confess that Jesus Christ came in the flesh is antichrist"; and anyone who does not confess the testimony of the cross is "of the devil"; and anyone who perverts the sayings of the Lord to suit "his own lusts" and says that there is neither a resurrection nor a judgement—that man is the first-born of Satan! [55]

Polycarp's conviction was that only the just will be raised ("'he who raised him' from the dead 'will also raise us' if 'we do his will'")[56], and it reinforced his moral exhortations; in his concluding blessing he prayed that "the God and 'Father of our Lord Jesus Christ,' give to you 'a lot and portion' with 'his saints,' and to us along with you, and to 'all men who are

---

[54] *Pol. ad phil* 2.1-2. All quotations from the *Letter* of Polycarp and the *Martyrdom of Polycarp* are taken from W.R. Schoedel, *The Apostolic Fathers: a New Translation and Commentary*, vol. 5 (Camden, N.J.,: Thomas Nelson and Sons, 1967).

[55] *Pol. ad Phil* 7.1.

[56] *Pol. ad Phil* 2.2.

under heaven who will believe in our Lord Jesus Christ' and in his 'Father who raised him from the dead.'"[57]

Underlying Polycarp's letter, and sometimes made explicit, was an effort to instil courage at the prospect of martyrdom:

> [Be persuaded] that "all these [martyrs] 'did not run in vain," but "in faith and righteousness," and that they are "in their due place beside the Lord with whom they also suffered." For they did not "love the present world" but "him who died for us and was raised by God because of us."[58]

It was Polycarp's own martydom that inspired the earliest of the *Acts* of the martyrs, probably written ca 155, almost half a century after his death, by an unknown author. Part of the long speech ascribed to Polycarp as he faced death is a thanksgiving.

> "I bless you"
> because "you have considered me worthy" of this day and
>   hour
> to receive "a portion, among the number" of the martyrs,
> in the "cup" of "your Christ"
> unto the resurrection of eternal life
> "both of soul and body"
> in the "incorruption" of the Holy Spirit.... [59]

[57] *Pol. ad Phil* 12.2.
[58] *Pol. ad Phil* 9.2.
[59] *Mart.* 14.2.

The Letter of Barnabas and the
Fragments of Papias

The writings examined thus far have been of a predominantly parenetic and polemic character, concerned to urge the practice of the christian life and to repudiate deviation of conduct or doctrine. Any mention of the resurrection has been subordinated to these concerns, sometimes to exhort confidence in divine justice and faithfulness, sometimes, combatting doceticism, to stress the physical reality of Christ's body, risen as well as historical. One inference that can be drawn from this subordination is that the promise of a risen life with Christ was such an immediate part of the faith of these writers that it needed no discussion in itself. The writings to be considered now have a more evident interest in eschatology, but it is still far from being their primary concern. Although one might expect that interest would have resulted in a more evident focus on the resurrection of the Christian than we have met so far, such, in fact, was not the case. Both these writings, however, display a certain millenarian expectation. Millenarianism has its classic expression in the Old Testament in Isaiah 65:17-25 and in the New Testament in 1 Corinthians 15:23b-28 and in Revelation 20:1-6. It looks forward to a reign of Christ of a thousand years between his second coming and the final resolution of all things. The millenarians assumed that part of the reward of the just would be to share in this triumph of Christ, and to do so effectively they would have to be materially embodied. In the *Letter of Barnabas* (and also in the *Didache*) we see only preliminary sketches of the expectation; full development would come with Irenaeus.

It has frequently been pointed out how much early christian eschatology in general borrowed its imagery from both the prophecies of the Old Testament and contemporary jewish apocalyptic. O'Hagan reminds us that "the promise, the land, final repose, the fruitfulness of the last times, the gathering together, the levelling for the just, the faithful remnant, the heavenly city and temple, the holy mountain" were all Old Testament images taken over by the early church and that all apocalyptic literature had the idea of reward for the just on a reconstituted earth.[60] The *Letter of Barnabas*, which is concerned more than any other of the writings of the sub-apostolic age with the refutation of Judaism, therefore puts strong emphasis on the late jewish theme of the judgment which will accompany the parousia.

> The Lord will judge the world impartially. Each man will receive payment in accord with his deeds—if he was good, his righteousness precedes him; if he was wicked, the reward of wickedness goes before him![61]

The reward of the righteous is a new creation, and certain passages in *Barnabas* indicate that its author shared the view of Ignatius and the author of the *Didache* that the new creation had already begun:

> Again, I will show you how he says to us that he made a second fashioning in the last times. And the Lord says: "Behold make the last things like the first." It is for this reason, therefore, that the prophets proclaimed: "Enter into the land flowing with milk and honey, and exercise lordship over it." See, then, we have been fashioned anew! As he says again in another prophet: "Behold," says the Lord, "I will remove from them—that is, from those on whom he foresaw the Lord's spirit—their stony hearts, and I will insert fleshly hearts." Because he was about to be manifested in the flesh and to dwell in us. For my brethren, our heart being thus inhabited constitutes a holy Temple to the Lord!.... Therefore we are those whom he conducts into the good land![62]

To some extent, therefore, the 'good land' has already come, but the promise of the future resurrection is equally clear in

[60]O'Hagan, 9.
[61]*Barn.* 4.12.
[62]*Barn.* 6.13-16.

the letter, and we find it linked here more explicitly with the death and resurrection of Christ than with his parousia.

> The prophets, after they had received special insight from him, prophesied concerning him. And he submitted so that he might break the power of Death and demonstrate the resurrection from the dead—thus it was necessary for him to be manifested in flesh. Also [he submitted] so that he might fulfill the promise to the fathers and, while he was preparing the new people for himself and while he was still on earth, to prove that after he has brought about the resurrection he will judge.[63]

It is not easy to put together a consistent account of Barnabas' eschatological vision; it has, in fact, been suggested that he combined two not entirely coherent traditions.[64] He clearly envisaged a thousand year interval after the six thousand years of this world (corresponding to the six days in which everything is to be completed).

> "And he resteth on the seventh day." He is saying this: When his Son comes he will put an end to the time of the Lawless One, and judge the impious, and change the sun and moon and stars—then he will truly rest "on the seventh day".... Further, he says to them: "I cannot bear your new moon celebrations and sabbaths." See how he is saying that it is not your present sabbaths that are acceptable to me, but that [sabbath] which I have made, in which, when I have rested everything, I will make the beginning of the eighth day—that is, the beginning of another world. Wherefore also we observe the eighth day as a time of rejoicing, for on it Jesus arose from the dead and, when he had appeared, ascended into the heavens.[65]

63 *Barn.* 5.6-7.
64 O'Hagan, 135.
65 *Barn.*, 15.5, 8-9.

The seventh day will be the day for judging 'the godless' and so will be preceded by the resurrection.

> Therefore it is fitting that when one has learned the ordinances of the Lord—as many as have been written— he walks in them. For he who does these things will be glorified in God's Kingdom; he who chooses those will perish with his works. For this reason there is a resurrection, for this reason there is recompense.... The day is near in which all things will perish together with the Wicked One. The Lord is near, and his reward.[66]

In summary, then, Barnabas appeared to hold that Christ will raise the dead, just and unjust, to judgement on the seventh day, that there will be a re-creation (which is to some degree already present) and that the eighth day will see it fully realized and as well Christ's manifestation and ascension. It would seem that, if the re-creation is to include a thousand year reign of Christ, it will occupy the seventh 'day' of a thousand years after the judgment and before Christ's glorification.

The most explicit and enthusiastic expression of millenarian hope in this period is found in the fragments ascribed to Papias, identified by Irenaeus as a disciple of John the apostle, (an identification that has provoked considerable discussion[67]). Irenaeus was pleased to have such an early, and therefore prestigious, endorsement of his own views, but Eusebius, describing Papias as teaching "a certain period of a thousand years after the resurrection from the dead when Christ's kingdom will be established physically upon this earth of ours," says that he misunderstood the apostolic accounts, taking them literally, rather than metaphorically, as they were intended.[68]

Irenaeus quotes Papias thus

---

[66] *Barn.* 21.1,3.

[67] Cf. e.g. Schoedel, 89-123.

[68] *Historia Ecclesiastica* 3.39.11-13.

[The blessings of Genesis 27:28-29 refer to the time] when creation, renewed and liberated, will bear an abundance of every kind of food "from the dew of heaven and the fertility of the earth"; thus the elders who saw John, the disciple of the Lord, recalled having heard from him how the Lord used to teach concerning those times and say [there follows a description of overflowing abundance when] all the animals using foods which are produced by the earth will live peacefully and harmoniously together fully subject to man.[69]

It is evident that the risen human body which is envisioned enjoying such a material paradise must itself be physical, but this was not the universal belief of Christians. The question of the nature of the resurrection body would soon move to the centre of patristic discussion of the afterlife.

[69] *A.H.* V.33.3.

3. THE APOLOGISTS

The Apologists wrote in the latter half of the second century for an audience very different than that of their predecessors, and in a very different genre. The Apostolic Fathers had been largely concerned with matters internal to the christian community (occasionally doctrinal, more usually relating to morality and church order), but the Apologists attempted to establish communication with those outside the church—its jewish and pagan despisers. The most notable theological contribution of the Apologists in the long term was the elaboration of a *logos* christology (Justin, Theophilus), but, more immediately, the greater part of their efforts was devoted to convincing graeco-roman society of the high standards of christian morality and the credibility of christian doctrine. An important part of this latter argument was concerned with the fact and nature of the christian eschatological hope.

There was a widespread interest in eschatology in the latter half of the second century. We see it reflected in the large number of apocalyptic writings, in the revival of the expectation of the imminent parousia by the Montanists and in the controversy surrounding the christian teaching of the resurrection. Although the delay of Christ's second coming seems not to have excited the same concern in the era of the Apologists as it had a century earlier, the parousia did continue to figure in christian thought, but now frequently in a millenarian context.

Like all apologetic arguments, those of the second century were very much shaped by the nature of their audience. Nowhere is this clearer than in the writings of Justin, where we can compare his different approaches to the Jew, Trypho, and the pagan emperor (and through him to all educated Romans),[1] but it is apparent in the writing of Athenagoras and Theophilus as well. The needs and expectations of different audiences were not, however, the only reasons that no one coherent eschatological picture emerges from this period. There were fundamental differences of opinion among Christians themselves concerning the worth of the material world, the relationship between body and soul, the nature of the eschatological kingdom and—tied in with all these—the meaning of resurrection. Not all the writings of the Apologists survive, and not all that have survived discuss these questions, but evidence of these differences will be discernible in the works of the writers to be examined in this chapter and the next—the Apologists, the Gnostics and the chief opponents of the Gnostics, Irenaeus and Tertullian.[2]

The lines between orthodoxy and heresy were not sharply defined in the second half of the second century, and the writings of Irenaeus and Tertullian at the end of the century were as important in forming future mainstream christian thinking on the subject of the resurrection as were those of Justin and Theophilus in christology. Before their time the situation was far from clearcut. Just as the Montanists were convinced that they alone were true to the eschatology of the primitive church which had looked for an imminent parousia, so both Tatian (apparently on the fringes of Gnosticism) and the author of the gnostic *Treatise on the Resurrection* (addressed to Rheginos) were equally sure that their 'spirit-

[1]Cf. L.W. Barnard, *Justin Martyr, his Life and Thought* (Cambridge: Cambridge University Press, 1967).

[2]I have chosen Justin, Theophilus, Athenagoras and Tatian as representative of the main strands of second century thought.

ual' interpretation of the New Testament writings, especially those of Paul, was the correct one.

Justin

Justin offered a twofold apologetic for the christian
eschatological hope, one in the *Dialogue with Trypho*,
another in the two *Apologies* ascribed to him. The former
was evidently tailored to the religious world of the jewish
community, the latter to that of the roman, and they are of
interest in representing two strands of christian thought on
the topic in the mid-second century.

In the *Dialogue with Trypho* (which is less a 'dialogue'
than an *apologia* and polemic) Justin's primary focus of
interest was the second coming of Christ and his millenarian
kingdom, and his chief weapon was the interpretation of the
Old Testament prophecies. First, however, Justin related
how it was that he shared so many of the basic religious
beliefs of his jewish interlocutor. The reader is told of his
futile search for wisdom among the philosophers (the description brings to mind Augustine's intellectual journey
two centuries later), a search which acquainted Justin with
the notion of cosmological cycles, punctuated by conflagra-
tions but without prospect of anything new. He was also
taught by the philosophers that the soul is immortal by
nature because it partakes in some way of the divine.
Neither of these teachings, nor others he examined, satisfied
him. Justin told Trypho how he was helped in his difficulties
by a mysterious old man, by means of whose skillful questioning he was led to assert that God can be seen only with
the eyes of the soul (seen more easily if that soul is not
encumbered by a body), and that it is not because of any
natural affinity with the divine that souls see God, but
because of the righteousness they may possess.

The *Dialogue* then continues with what has been described as the first christian attempt to discuss the immortal-

ity of the soul.[3] It is argued that souls must have a beginning, otherwise they could not sin (that is, sin is mutability, a concomitant of finitude). But the very fact that souls have a beginning, the Old Man points out, shows that they are not immortal in their own right, as Justin had been told.

> The soul either is life or it possesses life. If it is life, it would cause something other than itself to exist, just as motion causes something other than itself to move. Now, no one would deny that the soul lives; and if it lives, it does not live as life itself, but as a partaker of life. But, that which partakes of anything is different from that of which it partakes. Now, the soul partakes of life because God wishes it to live; it will no longer partake of life whenever God does not wish it to live.[4]

The soul, once in existence, the Old Man continues, never perishes; if it did, "this would certainly be of benefit to sinners."

> What happens to them? The souls of the devout dwell in a better place, whereas the souls of the unjust and the evil abide in a worse place, and there they await the judgement day. Those, therefore, who are deemed worthy to see God will never perish, but the others will be subjected to punishment as long as God allows them to exist and as long as he wants them to be punished.[5]

Later in the treatise Justin explains that it was the divine intention that human persons live eternally, and therefore God created human souls immortal. The freedom from suffering and death depended, however, on obedience to God's commandments, and disobedience brought death.

---

[3] Cf. J.A. Fischer, *Studien zum Todesgedanken in der alten Kirche* (Munich: M. Hueber, 1954), 153f.

[4] *Dial.* 6. All quotations from Justin's works are taken from T.B. Falls, *St. Justin Martyr* (New York; Christian Heritage, 1948), slightly altered.

[5] *Dial.* 5.

All human persons since Adam's fall would be subject to decay if they were not kept in existence by God, to be rewarded finally with eternal life or to be punished and then annihilated.[6]

If the philosophers have not the correct answers, Justin asks the Old Man, where can he turn? To the prophets of the Old Testament, is the reply.

> Their writings are still extant, and whoever reads them with the proper faith will profit greatly in his knowledge of the origin and end of things, and of any other matter that a philosopher should know.... [The events of the christian dispensation] that have taken place and are now taking place force you to believe their words.[7]

After further instruction, the Old Man goes on his way, leaving Justin to meditate on his words and become a Christian. It is against this background of having been brought to Christianity and to the recognition of Jesus as the true Messiah through a correct understanding of the jewish prophecies that Justin begins his discussion with a Jew, Trypho, and his friends. When the conversation turns to eschatology he employs concepts familiar to Judaism, stressing the christian belief in the second coming of the Messiah and his millenarian kingdom. After a description of the parousia taken largely from the book of Daniel,[8] Justin contrasts its glory with the misery of the Messiah's first coming, pointing out that both were known to the jewish prophets.

> It was also foretold by the Patriarch Jacob...that there would be two advents of Christ, and that in the first he would be subject to suffering, and that after this advent you people would have neither prophet nor king, and that

[6] *Dial.* 5.
[7] *Dial.* 7,
[8] *Dial.* 31.

the Gentiles who believe in the suffering Christ would look forward to his second coming.[9]

This first prophecy has been fulfilled, he reminds Trypho, and the second will be as well. Later in the treatise Justin describes the part the faithful will be given in that second coming, and its relationship to their attitude to the first:

> ...Christ has come in his power from the almighty Father,...calling all men to friendship, benediction, repentance and community, which should take place in the same land of all the saints [Canaan], of which he has pledged that there shall be an allotted portion for all the faithful.... Wherefore, men from every land, whether slaves or free men, who believe in Christ and recognize the truth of his words and those of the Prophets, fully realize that they will one day be united with him in that land, to inherit imperishable blessings for all eternity.[10]

When Trypho asks Justin to "prove...that [Christ] arose from the dead and ascended into heaven," Justin replies with a catena of Old Testament prophecies which have been fulfilled in that resurrection.[11] And, furthermore, Christians "believe that one day God will raise us up again through Christ and will make us free forever from corruption, pain, and death."[12] But nowhere does Justin explain the phrase 'through Christ' which links his resurrection with that of the Christian.

Will the just of the Old Testament, Trypho asks, "live again together with Jacob, Enoch and Noah in the resurrection of the dead?" Justin replies:

> since they who did those things which are universally, naturally and eternally good are pleasing to God, they

[9] *Dial.* 52.
[10] *Dial.* 139.
[11] *Dial.* 63
[12] *Dial.* 46.

shall be saved in the resurrection, together with their righteous forefathers. . . [and] with those who believe in Christ, the Son of God, who existed before the morning star and the moon, yet deigned to become incarnate, and be born of this virgin of the family of David, in order that by this dispensation he might conquer the serpent, that first sinner, and the angels who followed his example, and that he might thwart death and bring it to an end, so that, at the second advent of Christ, it would no longer have any power over those who believe in him and live according to his principles. At this second advent of Christ, some will be condemned to suffer eternally in the fires of hell, while others will be eternally free from suffering, corruption, and sorrow.[13]

The same promise cannot, however, be held out to those of Justin's day who, though believing "that the crucified Jesus is the Christ of God," continue to follow the mosaic law which is "in no way conducive to acts of justice and piety."[14]

In answer to Trypho's question, "do you really believe that this place Jerusalem shall be rebuilt, and do you actually expect that you Christians will one day congregate there to live joyfully with Christ, together with the patriarchs, the prophets, the saints of our [jewish] people and those who became proselytes before your Christ arrived?"[15], Justin acknowledges that not all "pure and pious Christians" hold the expectation of the millenarian kingdom shared with the Jews, but he is insistent that

> I and every other completely orthodox Christian feel certain that there will be a resurrection of the flesh, followed by a thousand years in the rebuilt, embellished, and enlarged city of Jerusalem, as was announced by the prophets Ezechiel, Isaiah and the others.[16]

[13] *Dial.* 45.
[14] *Dial.* 46.
[15] *Dial.* 80.
[16] *Dial.* 80.

It should be noted that Justin's belief was in a resurrection of the *flesh* as a corollary of millenarianism, and that he could insist on the millenarian hope as necessary component of orthodoxy is an indication of the doctrinal fluidity spoken of earlier, for these expectations were not as widely shared nor as integral a part of the church's teaching as Justin seems to have thought. It is evident that the millenial hope involves the resurrection of the flesh, on the other hand, the Old Man had spoken of the souls of the just and the unjust awaiting the judgement day, and Justin later in the treatise puts forward the idea of the survival of the soul after the death of the body, using as his proof text the Witch of Endor's invocation of Samuel's soul.[17] It would seem that Justin envisaged that, after this period of time, there would be the resurrection of all to judgement, the reign of the just with Christ for a thousand years and the punishment of the unjust for as long as God sees fit. Elsewhere in the *Dialogue*, however, he wrote as if the kingdom and the punishment will be eternal.

> But those filthy garments [falsehoods], which you place upon all those who by the name of Jesus embrace Christianity, will be thrown off us when he raises all of us, and makes some incorruptible, immortal, and free from pain in an everlasting and indissoluble kingdom, and banishes others into the eternal torment of fire.[18]

It has been suggested that Justin retains two eschatological traditions and that it is probably futile to look for too rigid a consistency, even within one treatise.[19]

The argumentation of the *Dialogue with Trypho* was that Justin thought most likely to reach jewish ears; the appeal to the hebrew prophets, the promise of a rebuilt Jerusalem and

[17] *Dial.* 105.

[18] *Dial.* 117.

[19] Cf. e.g. L.W. Barnard, "Justin Martyr's Eschatology," *Vigiliae Christianae* 19 (1965), 86-98.

a messianic kingdom. Predictably, in the first *Apology*, written somewhat later for the emperor, Antoninus Pius, although the Old Testament prophets are advanced as witnesses to the truth of Christianity, the thrust of the argument is different. There is no reference to a millenarian kingdom, and, for obvious reasons, hope of a "human kingdom" is explicitly rejected: "We mean a kingdom which is with God."[20] A promise of a millenarian kindgom would have spoken to no roman tradition, and so in the *Apology* the stress is on the eschatological promise of "an eternal and good life" and the punishment of "the pangs of torment eternally."[21]

The *Apology* opens by demanding justice for Christians, rejecting the charges brought against them, and explaining their beliefs and worship:

> We are desirous of an eternal and good life; we strive for the abode of God, the Father and Creator of all... We declare that [a judgement] will take place, but that it will be Christ who will assign the punishment to sinners. And in their very bodies, reunited to their souls, they will endure the pangs of torment eternally, and not only for a period of one thousand years, as Plato said.[22]

Justin argues that the Romans should have no difficulty with the notion of survival after death because their own practices presume it.

> Let the oracles of the dead and the sorcery you perform through innocent children, and the invoking of the souls of the dead, let those whom the magicians call dream-sending and familiar spirits, and let whatever else is performed by those skilled in such arts convince you that

[20]*I Apol.* 11.
[21]*I Apol.* 8.
[22]*I Apol.* 8.

even after death souls remain in a state of sensibility. Be convinced, likewise...by the teaching of the writers Empedocles and Pythagoras, Plato and Socrates, and by the ditch of Homer, and by the descent of Ulysses to see the dead, and by those who told similar stories. Treat us, therefore, in a similar manner as you treat them, for we believe in God not less, but more than they do, since we expect that our own bodies, even though they should be dead and buried in the earth, will be revived; for we claim that nothing is impossible with God.[23]

The theme of the power of God is the one that Justin pursues the most in this apologetic because it is an argument which finds points of contact in the pagan mind. Responding to the objection that the material body cannot be reconstituted, he asks if resurrection from the dead is any less credible than the beginning and development of human life.

And what would seem more incredible to a thinking person than if we were not in a body and someone were to affirm that from a little drop of the human seed it were possible to shape bones, muscles and flesh into the human form we now see? Now let us make this supposition: if you yourselves had not the form you now have, and were not born of parents like yours, and someone were to show you the human seed and the painted picture of a man, and were to affirm that from such a seed such a being could be produced, would you believe him before you saw the actual production? No one would dare deny [that you would not]. In like manner, because you have never witnessed a dead person rise again to life, you refuse to believe.... [S]o now realize that it is not impossible that human bodies, after they are dead and disseminated in the earth like seeds, should at the appointed time, at God's command, arise and assume immortality.... We [Christians] have learned that it is better to

[23]*I Apol.* 18.

believe what is impossible to our own nature and to men than, like other men, to be unbelievers, for we know that our Teacher, Jesus Christ, has said: 'What is impossible with men, is possible with God.'[24]

Justin goes on to point out parallels between pagan beliefs and christian ("we propose nothing new or different"[25]), including the roman teaching of deified emperors and those said to have risen from their funeral pyres.[26] It is, however, not the parallels to pagan teachings which make the christian doctrines credible, but the fact that they are true is due to their source: "We learned them from Christ and the prophets who preceded him."[27] A long description of christian beliefs and moral teachings follows, with considerable attention given to the reliability of the jewish prophets (a point Justin did not have to make with Trypho) and their foretelling the second coming of Christ in judgement. A typical passage, emphasizing the contrast between the two comings, reads

> Now, since we show that all those things that have happened had been foretold by the prophets before they happened, it must of necessity also be believed that those things which were likewise foretold, but are yet to happen, shall with certainty come to pass.... The prophets have foretold two comings of Christ: the one, which already took place, was that of a dishonoured and suffering man; the other coming will take place, as it is predicted, when he shall gloriously come from heaven with his angelic army, when he shall also raise to life the bodies of all the men that ever were, shall cloak the worthy with immortality, and shall relegate the wicked,

[24]*I Apol.* 19.
[25]*I Apol.* 21.
[26]*I Apol.* 21.
[27]*I Apol.* 23.

subject to sensible pain for all eternity, into the eternal
fire together with the evil demons.[28]

It is understandable that, writing to the pagan persecutors
of the Christians, Justin's repeated emphasis should be on
the eschatological judgement of the wicked. This theme
finds a context in his second *Apology*, addressed to the
roman Senate on the occasion of the execution of three
Christians. Those responsible for the deaths were under the
influence of demons, he says, but this does not free them
from responsibility for their actions. Justin cleverly links his
belief in the reality of eternal punishment with his demand
for justice to place the Romans in a cleft stick: if the eternal
punishment of sinners is not a fact either there is no God or
only a God indifferent to human right and wrong, and, if the
latter is the case, rulers have no moral authority.

> Since God, from the very beginning, created the race of
> angels and men with free will, they will justly pay the
> penalty in everlasting fire for the sins they have commit-
> ted.... The truth of this is shown everywhere by those
> legislators and philosophers who, acting according to
> right reason, have ordered some things to be done and
> others to be avoided.... Lest any one repeat the mistake
> of those so-called philosophers who claim that our state-
> ments that sinners are punished in everlasting fire are just
> boastful words calculated to instill terror, and that we
> want men to live a virtuous life through fear, and not
> because such a life is pleasant, I will make this brief reply,
> that if it is not as we say, then there is no God; or, if there
> is a God, he is not concerned with men, and virtue and
> vice are nothing, and legislators unjustly punish the
> transgressors of their excellent precepts.[29]

The Romans (who accused the Christians of atheism) could

---

[28] *I Apol.* 52.
[29] *II Apol.* 7 and 9.

not admit the first alternative, nor the second, which would undermine the legal foundations of the roman state. Unless they were prepared to admit that their system of justice has no divine foundation, they had to admit eternal punishment for the wicked. Justin goes on to argue just laws are in fact made through the instruction of the Word, but that "the bad angels made laws suited to their own iniquity, which are pleasing to their counterparts among men."[30] The implication was, of course, that Christians are not obliged to obey bad laws and that those who promulgate and enforce them will be punished.

> Be ashamed and blush, you who accuse the innocent of the very crimes [ritual murder, sodomy and sinful relations with women] you yourselves openly commit; and things of which you and your gods are guilty, you charge to those persons who have not the slightest part in them. Change your ways and come to your senses.[31]

In summary, then, Justin, in writing to the Jews, appeals to their hopes of the eschatological kingdom of God and tries to show that the christian expectation was the better founded because of their acceptance of the Messiah. To the Romans his argument is that of divine justice and the power of God. To both he affirms the christian belief in the resurrection of the body, or—more explicitly—of the flesh, in the context of the millenarian reign of Christ and the faithful.

Theophilus

We find in Theophilus of Antioch's treatise, *To Autolycus*, many of the themes already encountered in Justin, but there are significant differences as well. Like Justin, he believed that human beings were created neither mortal nor

---

[30]*II Apol.* 9.
[31]*II Apol.* 12.

immortal, but in the neutral state capable of either, that death is a consequence of sin and that the promised renewed life is a gift of God's love and mercy. The treatise was written to a pagan, and idol-worshipper, and there is in it no explicit allusion to Christ. When Theophilus argues in favour of the resurrection, he does so exclusively on the basis of reasons which might be credible to the pagan mind, i.e. those taken from the natural order, from divine power or from commonly held beliefs.

He begins by making a point similar to one made by Justin—that God can be seen only by the eyes of faith, cleansed of sin.

> You speak of [God], O man; you breathe his breath; you do not know him. This has happened to you because of the blindness of your soul and your heart, but if you will you can be cured. Deliver youself to the physician, and he will couch the eyes of your soul and heart. Who is the physician? He is God, who heals and gives life through *Logos* and *Sophia*. . . . If you know these things, O man, and live in purity, holiness and righteousness, you can see God. . . . When you put off what is mortal and put on imperishability, then you will rightly see God. For God raises up your flesh immortal with your soul; after becoming immortal you will then see the Immortal, if you believe in him now.[32]

Theophilus appeals to human faith in the natural order and human personal trust to support his argument for the resurrection is based on trust in God.

> If, then, the farmer trusts the earth and the sailor the ship and the sick man the physician, do you not want to entrust yourself to God, when you have received so many pledges from him? The first pledge is that he created you,

---

[32]*Aut.* 1.7. All quotations from Theophilus are taken from R.M. Grant, *Ad Autolycum* (Oxford: Clarendon Press, 1970).

bringing you from non-existence to existence.... He formed you out of a small, moist matter and a tiny drop, which itself previously did not exist. It was God who brought you into this life. Second, you believe that statues made by men are gods and work miracles. Then do you not believed that the God who made you can later make you over again?[33]

He then reminds his readers of the pagan belief in the life after death of Heracles and Asclepius; how can Autolycus deny that the dead are raised? But, aware, perhaps, of the flimsiness of this comparison, Theolphilus turns again to the natural order to demonstrate the trustworthiness of God.

God has given you many indications for believing him. If you will, consider the termination of the seasons and days and nights and how they die and rise again. And what of the resurrection of seeds and fruits, occurring for the benefit of mankind? One might mention that a grain of wheat or of other seeds when cast into the earth first dies and is destroyed, then is raised and becomes an ear.... "All these things the *Sophia* of God works" [1 Col 12:11] in order to demonstrate, even through these, that God is powerful enough to bring about the general resurrection of all men.[34]

Similarly, later in the treatise, Theophilus writes of the resurrection as signified in the variety of trees which spring from small seeds.

For what person who considers [them] will not marvel that a fig tree comes into existence from a fig seed, or that very great trees grow from other tiny seeds.[35]

[33]*Aut.* I.8.
[34]*Aut.* I.13.
[35]*Aut.* II. 14.

Theophilus understands the pagan difficulties because, he admits, he had not always believed in the resurrection. But he was brought to belief by reading the Old Testament prophets.

> Because I obtained proof from the events which took place after being predicted, I "do not disbelieve but believe," in obedience to God. If you will, you too must obey him and believe him, so that after disbelieving now you will not be persuaded later, punished by eternal tortures.[36]

In the second book of the treatise Theophilus rejects that interpretation of Genesis 2:6-7 ("God...breathed the breath of life into [man's] face, and man became a living soul") which understands it to teach that the human soul is immortal by nature.[37] The case is rather that "man was created in an intermediate state, neither entirely mortal nor entirely immortal, but capable of either state."[38] But, "through disobedience man acquired pain, suffering, and sorrow, and finally fell victim to death."[39] Death, however, is not an unmitigated evil, it shatters the human person "so that in resurrection [man] may be found...spotless and righteous and immortal."[40]

If human persons had been created immortal, Theophilus warns, they might have thought that they were gods, and, if mortal, they might have blamed God for their death. Linking mortality to human sin is a reminder that death was earned.

> [Despite w]hat man acquired for himself through his neglect and disobedience, God now freely bestows [the

---

[36] *Aut.* I. 14.

[37] *Aut.* II.19.

[38] *Aut.* II.24, cf. II.27.

[39] *Aut.* II.25,

[40] *Aut.* II.26.

opposite] upon him through love and mercy when man
obeys him. For as by disobedience man gained death for
himself, so by obedience to the will of God whoever will
can obtain eternal life for himself. For God gave us a law
and holy commandments; everyone who performs them
can be saved and, attaining to the resurrection, can
"inherit imperishability."[41]

The pattern begun by Justin of meeting the pagans on their
own ground was continued by Theophilus and many of their
arguments became standard in the christian repertory.

Athenagoras

Athenagoras' treatise *On the Resurrection* is the earliest
specifically on the topic which survives, and opinion differs
as to whether it was intended for a christian or a pagan
audience.[42] The fact that Athenagoras (like Tatian and
Theophilus) made no mention of Christ indicates the latter,
as does also, perhaps, the use of the writings of the greek
scientist, Galen, to support the christian doctrine.

Athenagoras begins by advancing arguments "on behalf
of the truth. . . directed to those who disbelieve or dispute it"
(contrasted with arguments "concerning the truth. . . for
those who are well-disposed and receive the truth gladly").[43]
He therefore sets out to show that the christian teaching
about the resurrection is worthy of belief by demonstrating
both that it lies within the divine power to raise the human
body and that it is appropriate that God should do so.
Divine inability, if it existed, could not stem from lack of

---

[41] *Aut.* II.27.

[42] I have accepted the arguments of L.W. Barnard, rather than those of R.M.
Grant and W.R. Schoedel concerning the authorship and date of *De Resurrectione*. Cf. L.W. Barnard, "Athenagoras: *De Resurrectione*," *Studia Theologica* 30
(1976), 1-42, with bibliographical references.

[43] *Res.* 1.3. All quotations from Athenagoras are taken from W.R. Schoedel,
Legatio and *De Resurrectione* (Oxford: Clarendon Press, 1973).

knowledge of the whereabouts of the bodies of the dead.

> It is impossible for God. . . to be ignorant of the nature of
> our bodies which are destined to arise; he knows every
> part and member in their entirety. Nor indeed can he be
> ignorant as to where everything goes that decomposes
> and what part of the appropriate element receives what is
> decomposed and dissolved into its own kind.[44]

Nor does God lack the ability necessary to raise the human
body. Justin drew the parallel with conception, Athenagoras draws it with creation.

> As to power, the creation of our bodies shows that God's
> power suffices for their resurrection. For if when he first
> gave them form, he made the bodies of men and their
> principal constituents from nothing, he will just as easily
> raise them up again after their dissolution, however that
> may have taken place. For this is equally possible for
> him.[45]

Athenagoras goes on to argue that the divine power can
reassemble bodies lost at sea or devoured by wild beasts (or
even cannibalized). He was the first christian writer to introduce (in lengthy and graphic detail) the notion of 'chain
consumption' (humans eating beasts which have eaten
humans), but was able to conclude that, no matter what
violence the dead body has suffered,

> After [the parts of the bodies devoured by beasts and
> eaten again by humans] have been separated again from
> the elements by the wisdom and power of him who links
> every kind of animal with its appropriate properties, they
> reunite intimately, one part with the other, even though
> they may be consumed by fire, rotted away by water,

[44] *Res.* 2.5.
[45] *Res.* 3.1.

devoured by wild beasts or any animal that comes along, or have one part which has been cut off from the whole body and has decomposed before the others. They are united again to one another and occupy the same place as before so as to restore the harmonious composition of the body and effect the resurrection and the life of the body that has died and has totally decomposed.[46]

The length of Athenagoras' treatment of this topic indicates both the extent to which such practical objections to the idea of bodily resurrection were held and the material character of the resurrection body as Athenagoras imagined it.

If resurrection of the human body is not outside the power of God, the question then becomes whether God in fact wills to . Athenagoras argues that God would not do so only if it were an unjust or unworthy action.[47] There would be injustice: such an action would not harm those ranked above humankind (angels), or those lower in the scale of being, because these latter cannot even discern injustice. He continues:

And it certainly cannot be said that any injustice is to be seen in regard to the man himself who is resurrected. For he consists of soul and body, and no wrong is inflicted on either his soul or his body. No sensible person will say that man's soul is wronged, for otherwise he will unwittingly reject also our present life along with the resurrection; if the soul is not wronged now when it dwells in a corruptible and passible body, much less will it be wronged when it lives with an incorruptible and impassible one. Neither is the body wronged in any way; for if the corruptible body has not been wronged now when linked with a incorruptible soul, much less will the incorruptible body be wronged when linked with an incorruptible soul.[48]

[46] *Res.* 8.4.
[47] *Res.* 10.1.
[48] *Res.* 10.5.

Even less is the resurrection of the dead unworthy of God:

> Moreover one cannot say that it is a work unworthy of
> God to raise up and reconstitute a decomposed body; for
> if the lesser work—the making of a corruptible and passi-
> ble body—is not unworthy of God, how much more is the
> greater work—the making of an incorruptible and
> impassible body—not unworthy of God.[49]

Athenagoras then turns to the positive presentation of the
christian teaching of the resurrection. Human persons were
made for a purpose: "[God] did not make man in vain; for he
is wise and no work of wisdom is vain."[50] That purpose is
not simply the propagation of the species, as it is with
irrational animals. Dismissing any suggestion that humankind was created for God's use, or for the use of any created
being, Athenagoras concludes:

> God made man for his own sake and out of the goodness
> and wisdom which is reflected throughout creation. . . .
> [And he made him for immortal life because] the Maker
> has decreed an unending existence to those who bear his
> image in themselves, are gifted with intelligence, and
> share the faculty for rational discernment, so that they,
> knowing their Maker and his power and wisdom and
> complying with law and justice, might live without dis-
> tress eternally with the powers by which they governed
> their former life, even though they were in corruptible
> and mortal bodies.[51]

The hope of the resurrection is not a mere fable or delusion,
but is securely founded on the will of God.

> [W]e have put our confidence in an infallible security, the

---

[49] *Res.* 10.6.
[50] *Res.* 12.3.
[51] *Res.* 12.5-6.

will of our Creator, according to which he made man of an immortal soul and a body and endowed him with intelligence and an innate law to safeguard and protect the things which he gave that are suitable for intelligent beings with a rational life. We full well know that he would not have formed such an animal and adorned him with all that contributes to permanence if he did not want this creature to be permanent. The Creator of our universe made man that he might participate in rational life and, after contemplating God's majesty and universal wisdom, perdure and make them the object of his eternal contemplation, in accordance with the divine will and the nature alloted to him. The reason then for man's creation guarantees his eternal survival, and his survival guarantees his resurrection, without which he could not survive *as man*.[52]

Athenagoras has here in passing taken account of the question whether or not eternal human existence demands the resurrection of the body. It is precisely his point that it does, and he argues the point at length a little later in the treatise.

For if human nature universally considered is constituted by an immortal soul and a body which has been united with it at its creation; and if God has not separately assigned a creation and existence and course of life of this kind to the soul as such or to the body but to men who are made up of both, so that they might spend their life and come to one common end with the parts from which they are created and exist; then it is necessary, since all there is is one living being composed of two parts, under-going all the experiences of soul and body, and actively carrying out whatever requires the judgement of the senses and of reason, that the entire concatenation of such phenomena leads to one end so that all these things. . . might be fully integrated into one harmonious and concordant whole. If

[52]*Res.* 15.2-4.

there is one harmony and concord of the entire living being, including the things that spring from the soul and the things that are done by the body, then the end of all these phenomena must also be one. And the end will truly be one if the same living being whose end it is remains constituted as before. The living being will be genuinely the same if everything remains the same which serves as its parts. . . . [W]ithout [the resurrection] the same parts would not be united with one another in a way that conforms with their nature, nor would the same men be reconstituted as they were.[53]

Human persons are created to "discern intelligibles" (substances) and "the goodness, wisdom, and justice of him who endowed men with [understanding and reason]."[54] But, Athenagoras argues, because the objects of human knowledge are permanent, the knowledge should also be permanent, and this can happen only if the knower can attain immortality.

It is man—not simply soul—who received understanding and reason. Man, then, who consists of both soul and body must survive for ever; but he cannot survive unless he is raised. For if there is no resurrection, the nature of men *as men* would not be permanent. And if the nature of men is not permanent. . .vain is everything admirable implanted in men and effected by men, or rather, vain is the very creation and being of man. But if vanity in the works of God and the gifts granted by him is ruled out entirely, it is absolutely necessary that the body should be permanent in a way that conforms with its own nature and should exist eternally with the deathless soul.[55]

[53] *Res.* 15.2-4.
[54] *Res.* 15.5.
[55] *Res.* 15.6-8.

This integration of body and soul will be interrupted, Athenagoras admits, but death, the "concomitant of a needy and corruptible existence"[56] is best compared to sleep, both in the cessation of conscious life and in the awakening.

> The natural suspension of the senses and the native faculties in sleep also appear to interrupt the conscious life, when men go to sleep at regular intervals of time and, so to speak, return to life again. Yet we are not unwilling to call it the same life. That is why, I think, some call sleep the 'brother of death',.. because similar passive states affect both the dead and those asleep, at least in so far as they are tranquil, and are conscious of nothing that goes on around them or, rather, are not even conscious of their own existence of life. If then we are not unwilling to call that human life the same life which is filled with discontinuity from birth to dissolution and interrupted in the ways we have indicated above, then neither should we exclude the life which follows dissolution and ushers in the resurrection with it, even though it has been interrupted for a time by the separation of the soul from the body.[57]

Those raised from the dead will live incorruptibly. Such an expectation (of new life after death) is no more far-fetched, Athenagoras goes on to argue, than all the changes inherent in the development of the human person from conception to old age, yet which are confirmed by "the chain of natural events" and by reason as well.

> Still more so does reason, in seeking the truth on the basis of what naturally follows, confirm the resurrection, since it is more trustworthy and more secure than experience in providing confirmation of truth.[58]

[56] *Res.* 16.3.
[57] *Res.* 16.5-6.
[58] *Res.* 17.4.

Athenagoras then turns to what he calls "a secondary argument" for the resurrection that is the expectation of a just judgement. The first proof of the resurrection sprang from "the fact of creation," the second will be "from the investigation of the [human] end,"[59] that is, since the human person is rational, he or she requires justice.

> [I]t is necessary that such a man [made up of body and soul] should be held accountable for all his deeds and receive reward and punishment because of them. Just judgement requires the composite creature for his deeds. The soul alone should not receive the wages for deeds done in conjunction with the body...nor should the body alone be requited.... [I]t is man, the combination of both, who receives judgement for each of his deeds. Our inquiry finds that this does not happen in our life-time.... Nor does it happen after our death; for the composite creature no longer exists when the soul is separated from the body and when the body itself is again dispersed among the elements from which it came and no longer preserves anything of its previous form or shape, still less any memory of its actions. What follows is clear to everyone: that this corruptible and dispersible body must, according to the apostle, put on incorruptibility, so that, when the dead are revivified through the resurrection and what has been separated or entirely dissolved is reunited, each may receive his just recompense for what he did in the body, whether good or evil.[60]

Athenagoras amplifies the argument from judgement and goes on to that from final cause: "Every natural thing and every artifact must have an end that suits it."[61]

> [M]ankind's end must surely be distinguished from that

---

[59] *Res.* 18.1.
[60] *Res.* 18.4-5.
[61] *Res.* 24.2.

common to other creatures, since it has to do with a distinctive nature. Certainly it is not right to argue for the same end both for creatures who have no share in rational discrimination and for those who act in accordance with an innate rational law and can exercise prudence and justice.... If the end has to do with the composite, and if this cannot be discovered either while men are still alive here below...nor yet when the soul is in a state of separation...then the end of men must certainly be seen in some other state of the same composite creature.... Since this is the necessary consequence, there must surely be a resurrection of bodies that have died or even undergone complete dissolution, and the same men must rise again.... The same body cannot receive the same soul in any other way than by resurrection. When this takes place, the end that suits human nature is the result.[62]

Contemplation of God is the end appropriate to the human person, in Athenagoras' eyes, and it is within God's power and will to grant such an end. It is on these considerations that Athenagoras bases his confidence.

Tatian

The publication of the Nag Hammadi library has strengthened our perception of the importance to the early church of Gnosticism, both in itself and in the reactions it provoked. With the *Oration* of Tatian we are at least on the borders of that gnostic world and, according to some, in it. The accusation that Tatian was a Gnostic came initially from Irenaeus. who describes him as teaching the existence of a cosmos of invisible aeons, the sinfulnss of marriage and the damnation of Adam.[63] The justice of the accusation is still debated. Grant sees a "thoroughgoing gnosticism" in

[62]*Res.* 24.4; 25.2-3.
[63]*Adversus Haereses* I.28.1.

Tatian's writings, not only in the matters that Irenaeus pointed out, but also in the absence of any clear statement that the flesh is raised.[64] Barnard, however, points out that, while Tatian's eclectically inclined mind did pick up many gnostic themes, "in the mid-second century it was possible...to adopt certain gnostic ideas without putting [oneself] outside the Church."[65] Tatian's "views on God as Creator of matter, the incarnation of the Logos, and the Holy Spirit are not in any way gnostic."[66]

The *Oration to the Greeks* (the only writing of Tatian's, apart from fragments, that survives) is wide-ranging, polemical and disorganized. Death and resurrection are treated in several places, but in none systematically. Tatian sees human life as a double coming into existence from non-existence, not in the recurrent cycles of stoic thought, but as he describes here:

> It was through my birth that I, previously non-existent, came to believe that I did exist. In the same way, when I who was born, cease to exist through death...I shall once more be in my previous state of non-existence followed by birth.[67]

The initial non-existence was of both body and soul; the soul neither existed before the body nor is it immortal of its own nature. Tatian teaches that the human person was first created immortal, not with "the very nature of the good which is God's alone," but able to achieve good through free choice.[68] Adam's sin lost the more powerful spirit which gives life [to the soul] in the Word, that is, the image and

---

[64]R.M. Grant, "The Heresy of Tatian," *Journal of Theological Studies* 5 (1954), 62-68.

[65]L.W. Barnard, "The Heresy of Tatian—Once Again," *The Journal of Ecclesiastical History* 19 (1968), 1-10.

[66]Barnard, 7.

[67]*Grace*. 6. All quotations from Tatian are taken from M. Whittaker, *Tatian, Oratio ad Graecos and Fragments* (Oxford: Clarendon Press, 1982).

[68]*Graec*. 7.

likeness of God, and the human race became mortal. But there is hope[69]

> The soul... is not in itself immortal but mortal; yet it also has the power to escape death. For if it is ignorant of the truth it dies and is dissolved with the body, but rises later at the end of the world along with the body, to suffer death by immortal punishment.[70]

Tatian explains in the same passage that

> The [divine] spirit became originally the soul's companion, but gave it up when the soul was unwilling to follow it. The soul kept a spark, as it were, of the spirit's power, yet because of its separation it could no longer see things that are perfect, and so in its search for God went astray and fashioned a multitude of gods, following the demons and their hostile devices. God's spirit is not given to all, but dwelling among some who behaved justly and being intimately connected with the soul, [the divine spirit] revealed by predictions to the other souls what had been hidden. The souls which were obedient to wisdom attracted to themselves the kindred spirit, but those which were disobedient and rejected the servant of the suffering God were clearly shown to be enemies of God rather than his worshippers.[71]

The meaning of this passage is clearest if it is read as a soteriology with gnostic leanings, with the souls which were faithful to wisdom brought back to the Spirit, thus escaping eternal death. But even the faithful soul is "dissolved" on the death of the body, although it does not itself die "if it has obtained knowledge of God."[72] The soul ignorant of the

[69]*Graec.* 7.
[70]*Graec.* 13.
[71]*Graec.* 13.
[72]*Graec.* 13.

truth does, however, die, to rise again "later at the end of the world along with the body, to suffer death [again] by immortal punishment."[73] Tatian is saying that God grants a certain life apart from the body to the souls of the just, but it is clear that his understanding of normal and full life is that of the soul and body together.

Tatian uses the standard arguments to meet the frequently heard objections to the resurrection of the material body, the flesh.

> If fire consumes my bit of flesh, the vaporized matter is still contained in the world. If I am annihilated in rivers and seas, or torn to pieces by wild beasts, I am still stored in a rich lord's treasury.... God the ruler, when he wishes, will restore to its original state the substance that is visible only to him.[74]

God will restore the substance of the body because the soul and the body need each other: the flesh contains the soul, the soul is manifest through the body. "[The soul] can never appear by itself apart from the body, nor is the flesh resurrected apart from the soul."[75] Some say, Tatian points out, "that the soul is immortal," but he insists "that the piece of flesh joined with it is immortal too."[76] By 'immortal' Tatian clearly does not mean 'will not die,' but rather 'will live again without death.' It would appear, therefore, that the unqualified contention that Tatian shared the Gnostics' rejection of the resurrection of the body is mistaken. The question of the fact and nature of the resurrection body, however, continued to be hotly disputed.

[73]*Graec.* 6.
[74]*Graec.* 15.
[75]*Graec.* 25.
[76]*Graec.* 25.

4. THE REACTION TO
GNOSTICISM

It has been said of christian Gnosticism generally that it saw itself as "a reaffirmation, though in somewhat different terms" and as "the faithful continuation, under changing circumstances, of that original stance which made Christians Christians. But the 'somewhat different terms' and 'under changing circumstances' also involved real divergences, and other Christians surely considered Gnosticism a betrayal of the original Christian position."[1] Such an observation is particularly true of the gnostic interpretation of the resurrection, and the late second and early third centuries witnessed strong reactions to it. The point which distinguished Tatian's treatment of the resurrection from that now generally termed 'gnostic' was his attention to the physical body, his insistence that, although materially dispersed, it will be reconstituted and raised. It was precisely around this point—the physical nature of the risen body or, to put it another way, the raising of a physical body—that the battle between the christian Gnostics and their opponents raged from the second to the fourth centuries.

Christians, gnostic and non-gnostic alike, were agreed

[1]J.M. Robinson, ed., *The Nag Hammadi Library in English.* (San Francisco: Harper and Row, 1977), 4.

that the events described in the New Testament had taken place (although Gnostics tended to a docetic understanding of Jesus), they agreed also that Jesus was raised and that resurrection is the christian hope. But what did 'resurrection' mean and, in particular, how should 1 Corinthians 15:35ff be understood— "with what kind of body to [the dead] come?" Just as the Gnostics' view of the cosmos was such that they could not accept historical events as loci of salvation (but rather saw them as symbolizing "the process of redemption that occurs within those who perceive their inner meaning"[2]), so gnostic belief in the resurrection of the body was an expression of confidence in the eschatological communion of the 'pneumatics,' the spiritual Christians, with God. There were, of course, many varieties of Gnosticism, but all shared a tendency, if not to deny the resurrection of the body, at least to anticipate that that body would be immaterial. It was against valentinian Gnosticism that Irenaeus and Tertullian wrote, and the following passage from the *Apocryphon of John* represents one version of its teaching on the resurrection.

> And I said to the Savior, 'Lord will all the souls be brought then into the pure light?' He answered, 'Those on whom the Spirit of life will descend and (with whom) he will be with the power, they will be saved and become perfect and be worthy of the greatnesses and be purified in that place [a dwelling for the aeons] from all wickedness and the involvements in evil. Then they [will] have no other care than the incorruption alone, to which they [will] direct their attention from [that point] on, without anger or envy or jealousy or desire and greed of everything. They are not affected by anything except the state of being in the flesh alone, which they bear while looking expectantly for the time when they will be met by the receivers. Such then are worthy of the imperishable, eter-

[2]E. Pagels, *Th Johannine Gospel in Gnostic Exegesis.* (New York and Nashville: Abingdon, 1973) 14.

nal life and the calling. [When it has come out of its flesh] [t]he soul in which the power [of the Spirit is] will become superior to the despicable [material world]...[t]he soul is strong and she flees from evil and, through the intervention of the incorruptible one, she is saved and she is taken up to the rest of the aeons.[3]

The christian Gnostics' use of Paul, particularly of 1 Corinthians 15, in support of their understanding of the resurrection of the body is noteworthy. In an analysis of valentinian exegesis, Pagels has pointed out that their interpretative principle, here as elsewhere, was to refer apparently conflicting passages to different groups—the 'hylics' (those who belong to the race of matter), the 'psychics' (those who belong to the race of soul) and the 'pneumatics' (those who belong to the race of spirit).[4] Tertullian, in his presentation of the valentinian teaching, describes these groups as the carnal, who were doomed to destruction, the animal, who could choose between the material and the spiritual, and the spiritual, whose function it was to educate the animal.[5] He writes:

> [They say] that the animal (psychic) man has need of training in the sensible order, and that is why the plan of the world was prepared, and the Saviour made present in that world.... However, he had nothing of the material about him, inasmuch as [matter] is completely apart from salvation..... [They say] all this so that, the condition of our flesh being divorced from Christ, they thrust [it] away from hope of salvation.[6]

Thus, in this reading of 1 Corinthians 15:12-57 the 'dead'

---

[3] *The Apocryphon of John*, F. Wisse, trans., in *Nag Hammadi Library*, 112-113.

[4] E. Pagels, "The Mystery of the Resurrection," *Journal of Biblical Literature* 93 (1974), 276-88.

[5] *Adv. Val.* 29.

[6] *Adv. Val.* 26.

were the psychics who must be raised from the death of their present existence to the life the pneumatics enjoy; the psychic seed sown in dishonour would be raised to the glory of the pneumatic seed. Those who denied this teaching denied implicitly, the Gnostics argued, the raising of the body of Jesus and the soul of Christ to spiritual (pneumatic) life, and so their faith was in vain. This gnostic reading combined a realized and a future eschatology; the dead who have the seed of true gnosis live already totally in the Spirit, and, for the duration of the cosmos, the risen Christ (the first fruits of the psychic Christians) reigns with the demiurge; at the eschaton he "will raise all the psychics. . . and lead them into reunion with the pneumatic elect with the Father."[7] Tertullian describes their soteriology unsympathetically:

> The souls of the just (that is, our souls) will be carried to the Demiurge. . . . Nothing except the spiritual multitude of Valentine is admitted to the palace of the Pleroma. That is why here [on earth] the spiritual (that is, the inner] men at first divest themselves (to divest oneself is to put aside the soul with which one seems to be clothed), and return to their Demiurge those [souls] which they have obtained from it. They will become wholly intellectual spirits, beyond touch and sight, and thus invisibly they will be received into the Pleroma.[8]

Among the Nag Hammadi writings is a treatise on the resurrection which represents a school not far removed from that of the Valentinians. Assessments of the treatise vary from Layton's "a detailed and sympathetic exposition of a celebrated heresy attacked by the author of the pastoral epistles ('[those] who have swerved from the truth by holding that the resurrection is past already,' 2 Tim. 2:17),"[9] to

---

[7] *Adv. Val.* 32.

[8] *Adv. Val.* 32

[9] Bentley Layton, *The Gnostic Treatise on Resurrection from Nag Hammadi* (Missoula, Montana: Scholars Press, 1979), 1.

Peel's "[a treatise by] a late second century christian Gnostic whose views on several crucial points are closer to the apostle Paul than to the Valentinians."[10] Whether the treatise is characterized as valentinian Christianity or christian Valentinianism, it does seem to represent an attempt to bridge the gap between an unqualified affirmation of the resurrection of a material body and the apparent denial of any resurrection. The treatise was addressed by its anonymous author to his pupil, Rheginos, who had asked "pleasantly what is proper concerning the resurrection."[11] The instructor begins with the question, "How did the Lord make use of things while he existed in flesh?"[12] The response is that "he embraced...both the humanity and the divinity, so that on the one hand he might vanquish death through his being Son of God, and that on the other through the Son of Man, the restoration to the Pleroma might occur."[13] By 'Pleroma' the author understands the 'macrocosmic reality' of which the world is the polar opposite.[14] The treatise continues with the assertion that

> [the Word of Truth...has revealed] all things openly concerning existence—the destruction of evil on the one hand, but the revelation of the Elect on the other —this is the emanation of Truth and Spirit. Grace is that which belongs to Truth. The Savior swallowed up death...for he put aside the world which is perishing. He transformed [himself] into an imperishable Aeon and raised himself up, having swallowed the visible by the invisible, and he gave us the way of our immortality.... [I]f we are manifest in this world wearing him, we are that one's beams

[10] "The Treatise on Resurrection (I,4)," M. Peel. trans., *Nag Hammadi Library* 50-53; introduction.

[11] *Resurrection* 44.5-6. All quotations from *The Treatise on the Resurrection* are taken from Peel.

[12] *Resurrection* 44.14-15.

[13] *Resurrection* 44.28-52.

[14] L.H. Martin, "The Anti-philosophical Polemic and Gnostic Soteriology in 'The Treatise on the Resurrection'," *Numen* 20 (1973), 35.

and we are embraced in him until our setting, that is to say, our death in this life. We are drawn to heaven by him, like beams by the sun, not being restrained by anything. This is the spiritual resurrection which swallows up the psychic in the same way as the fleshly.[15]

What the author means by the spiritual resurrection 'swallowing up' the fleshly and the psychic is not entirely clear from this passage, but another makes it apparent that his understanding of resurrection included a 'spiritual' flesh, that is, the treatise is teaching neither the immortality of the soul entirely apart from the body nor the resurrection of the material earthly body.[16]

Therefore, never doubt concerning the resurrection, my son Rheginos. For if you did not exist in flesh, you received flesh when you entered this world. Why [then] will you not receive flesh when you ascend into the Aeon. What is better than the flesh is for it the cause of life. Is not that which comes into being on your account yours? Does not that which is yours exist with you?[17]

This resurrection flesh is not the earthly body revivified, but something which "is better than the flesh" and "the cause of life." A few lines further on, the treatise is more explicit:

[I]ndeed, the visible members which are dead shall not be saved, for (only) the living [members] which exist within them would arise.[18]

The treatise appears to affirm an immediate resurrection, although one commentator sees an ambiguity which reflects

[15] *Resurrection* 45.3-46.2.

[16] Cf. M. Peel, '*The Epistle to Rheginos*': *a Valentinian Letter on the Resurrection* (London: SCM, 1969), 146-48.

[17] *Resurrection* 47.2-13.

[18] *Resurrection* 47.38-48.3.

a certain eschatological tension within the treatise.[19] The treatise asserts:

> [T]here are some [who] wish to understand in the inquiry about those things they are looking into, whether he who is saved, if he leaves his body behind, will be saved immediately? Let no one be given cause to doubt concerning this....[20]

The author is anxious to dispel any notion that the restriction of the resurrection to the inner principle of life in any way denies its reality.

> What, then, is the resurrection? It is always the disclosure of those who have risen. For if you remember reading in the Gospel that Elijah appeared and Moses with him, do not think the resurrection is an illusion. It is no illusion, but it is truth. Indeed, it is more fitting to say that the world is an illusion, rather than the resurrection which has come into being through our Lord the Saviour, Jesus Christ.[21]

It is noteworthy that the resurrection of Christ is much more causally tied to the resurrection of the Christian in this treatise than in many of the others considered. Until now, when the link has been mentioned, it has been generally in the context of exemplar and guarantor. But here the Saviour "has swallowed up death," and "restored the Pleroma." It has been pointed out, however, that "the Cross is mentioned nowhere in [the] Letter, the salvation has to do with flight from a corruptible world rather than with reconciliation...to God."[22] Nor is judgement prominent in the trea-

---

[19]Peel (1969), 144.

[20]*Resurrection* 47.31-37.

[21]*Resurrection* 48.3-19.

[22]Peel (1969), 145.

tise,[23] and this is a marked departure from the earlier eschatological discussions. One might argue, however, that for this author, as for others, judgement preceded the resurrection that only the pneumatic and the psychic are raised, the first immediately, the second eventually. Unnik has concluded that this teaching on the resurrection was developed "to fit the gnostic conception of the Pleroma and the world,"[24] and that the 'drawing up' which constitutes at least that resurrection which immediately follows death repairs a cosmological, not a theological, 'misfortune.'[25] In any event, the whole schema was to be vigorously repudiated by Irenaeus and Tertullian.

Irenaeus

The first sustained anti-gnostic christian polemic which survives is that of Irenaeus. He argued vigorously for the resurrection of the material body, presenting as a foil an unnuanced representation of the gnostic teaching which described it as a total repudiation of any, even a spiritual, bodily resurrection. Recent scholarship has shown both the complexity of motives underlying Irenaeus' writings and the inaccuracy of his depiction of gnostic, particularly the valentinian, teaching.[26] He remains, nevertheless, an extremely important figure because the writings in which he countered gnostic eschatology were instrumental in fixing christian belief for centuries to come. Irenaeus' chief criticisms of gnostic eschatology sprang from his perception of its divisive elitism[27] and of its denial of the resurrection of

---

[23]W.C. Van Unnik, "The Newly Discovered Gnostic 'Epistle to Rheginos' on the Resurrection: I and II," *Journal of Ecclesiastical History* 15 (1964), 151.

[24]Van Unnik 165.

[25]Van Unnik 145.

[26]E. Pagels, *The Gnostic Gospels* (New York: Random House, 1979) and G. Vallee, "Theological and Non-theological motives in Irenaeus' Refutation of the Gnostics," in E. Sanders, *Jewish and Christian Self-definition* (Philadelphia: Fortress, 1980), vol. 1, 174-185.

[27]Vallee, 182.

the earthly body. He argued for the latter on the basis of a strongly positive creationist theology (a position in stark contrast with gnostic dualism) and of an equally strong expectation of a material millenarian kingdom.

Irenaeus had to meet the gnostic argument that the body, because it is material, is not susceptible of salvation.[28] His refutation is argued first on the basis of God's power, with the now familiar analogy between the first and second creation. Referring to the Gnostics, he writes:

> They refuse to acknowledge the power of God...who dwell upon the weakness of the flesh but do not consider the power of him who raises it from the dead. For, if God does not give life to what is mortal and does not recall the corruptible to incorruptibility, then he is not powerful. But that he is powerful in all these matters, we ought to know from a consideration of our origins, because God took a lump of earth and formed man. For indeed how much more difficult and hard it is to believe that someone made out of previously non-existent bones and nerves and veins and all the other things which pertain to man something which is a living and rational man than that he reconstituted what was made and thereafter dissolved in the earth.[29]

The disposition of the flesh to salvation had been demonstrated as well by the incarnation: "If the flesh were not in a position to be saved, the Word of God would in no wise have become flesh."[30] Citing several texts from the hebrew bible which cry to God for vengeance for blood shed, Ireneaus contends that

> [Christ] indicates the future recapitulation of the blood of all the just and prophets shed from the beginning in his

[28] *Adversus.Haereses.* 1.24.5; 1.27.3.
[29] *AH* V.3.2; cf. II.29.1f.
[30] *AH* V,14,1.

own person, and that he himself will ask for an accounting of this blood. Now this accounting could not be required unless [that blood] also was capable of being saved, nor would the Lord have recapitulated these things in himself unless he himself had been made of flesh and blood in the manner of the original formation, saving in his own person at the end that which has perished in the beginning in Adam.[31]

Furthermore, God's power in raising the body was exercised through Christ, as symbolized in his healing ministry.

For the Maker of the universe, the Word of God, who from the beginning formed man, when he found that which he had moulded ruined by wickedness, healed it in all possible ways.... For what was his object in healing the members of the flesh, and restoring them to their pristine condition, if they, having been healed by him, were not to obtain salvation?... For life is effected through healing and incorruption through life. Whoever, therefore, confers healing, confers life; and whoever gives life, also wraps his handiwork in incorruption.[32]

In Irenaeus' thought the human person is made up of flesh, soul and spirit, with soul understood in the now traditional way as not immortal by nature (that is not itself life, but partaking of life as long as God wills that it should) and spirit (as that which is of God and which mingles with the soul to form the spiritual and perfect person).[33] Of these three, death pertains only to the body, not to the spirit (because it is simple and cannot be destroyed), nor the soul (which continues to receive life from God).[34] In death the body returns to the earth from which it came and dissolves

[31]*AH* V.14.1; cf. III.5.3; V.7.1
[32]*AH* V.12.6.
[33]*AH* V.6.1.
[34]*AH* V.7.1.

there, But, as seed fallen to the ground, the body, having been nourished by the Eucharist, will be raised again by the word of God. Combining the argument from nature that was so frequently used with this understanding of the Eucharist, Irenaeus writes:

> And just as a cutting from the vine planted in the ground bears fruit in due season, and, as "a grain of wheat falling into the earth," once decomposed, rises increased many times by the Spirit of God who sustains all things, and then, through [human] skill, these things are put to the use of man, and, having been touched by the word of God, become the Eucharist, which is the body and blood of Christ, so also our bodies, nourished by the Eucharist and laid in the earth and decomposed there, will rise in due season, the Word of God granting them resurrection to the glory of God.[35]

In this passage it is the word/Word of God which effects the transformation of earthly wheat and earthly bodies. Earlier in the treatise we find the same parallel between the Eucharist and the resurrection of the body as two instances of material objects transformed, the first by invocation, the second by the reception of the body and blood of Christ.

> Again, how can [the Gnostics] say that flesh which is nourished by the body and blood of the Lord suffers [everlasting] corruption and does not receive life? Let them, therefore, either change their opinion, or refrain from presenting those theories which have been described. Our thinking is consonant with the Eucharist, and the Eucharist in turn confirms our thinking.... For just as bread which is produced from the earth, receiving the invocation of God is no longer ordinary bread, but the Eucharist, consisting of two elements, earthly and heav-

---

[35] *AH* V.2.3; cf. V.12.6.

enly, so our bodies, receiving the Eucharist, are no longer corruptible, having the hope of resurrection.[36]

In the context of his anthropology, Irenaeus sees the human spirit as open to the Spirit of God and thus the means of bringing the whole human person within the realm of that Spirit. He writes of the Holy Spirit as having been received as the pledge which makes the human person spiritual in anticipation, even in this life, and by which eventually all that which is now mortal will be made immortal.

> But now we receive some share of his Spirit, tending towards perfection and preparing [us] for incorruption by gradually accustoming us to grasp and bear God: [this preparation] the apostle called an earnest (in the letter he wrote to the Ephesians), that is part of that honour which God has promised to us.... Therefore, if this earnest now dwelling in us already makes us spiritual and if what is mortal is absorbed by immortality,.. and this is accomplished not by discarding the flesh, but by the communication of the Spirit...if, therefore, now posessing this earnest, we cry, 'Abba, Father,' what will it be like when, risen, we see him face to face?[37]

And, those who deny the possibility of the resurrection of the earthly body do not only deny divine power and the christian teaching of the incarnation, but repudiate Christ's resurrection as well.

> For the heretics, despising the handiwork of God and not accepting the salvation of their flesh, both contemptous of the promise of God and being wholly superior to God in their thought, say that, as soon as they die, they will pass beyond the heavens, and the Demiurge, and go to the Mother, or to that Father they have falsely phanta-

---

[36]*AH* IV,18,5; cf. IV.5.2.

[37]*AH* V.8.1; cf. V.10.2.

sized. Those who therefore reject the universal resurrection...do not choose to understand that, if matters are as they say, the very Lord himself, in whom they say they believe, did not effect his resurrection on the third day; but immediately upon dying on the cross, without delay ascended to heaven, leaving his body in the earth.[38]

Irenaeus argues as well from the comparability of human temporal life with life eternal.

If [the Gnostics] live now and if their whole body partakes of life, how do they dare say that flesh is not worthy of life, confessing that now they have life themselves? It is just as if someone, holding a sponge filled with water, or a flaming torch, were to say that the sponge could not partake of water nor the torch of fire.[39]

It is evident that Irenaeus is using the pauline writings extensively in his battle against Gnosticism, and this reappropriation of Paul by non-gnostic christianity is one of the most interesting features of Irenaeus' writings.[40] But it should be noted that, in the process, the 'transformed' body of 1 Corinthians 15 has become, explicitly, a revivified historical body.

Irenaeus was a strong millenarianist (as Barnabas and Justin had been before him), and this belief in an earthly kingdom between Christ's second coming and the eschaton was very much of a piece with his stress on the physical resurrection of the body. Millenarian hopes differed in detail, but in all there was a necessary insistence on the resurrection of the material body. As Christians in the second century pieced together an eschatological picture from a literal understanding of Old Testament prophecies of the messianic kingdom and from New Testament predic-

[38]*AH* V.31.1.

[39]*AH* V.3.3.

[40]Cf. E. Pagels, *The Gnostic Paul* (Philadelphia, Fortress, 1975).

tions of the return of Christ in glory, there arose an expectation of a glorious reign of the just with Christ, a time when
all wrongs would be redressed, justice would prevail, the
fruits of the earth would be plentiful, and even the animal
world would be at peace.[41]

Irenaeus' most complete description of the hoped for
kingdom comes in *Against the Heresies* V.26ff. Starting
with the predictions in the Book of Revelation of a brief
reign of the unrighteous with "the Beast," Irenaeus goes on
to the eternal kingdom, "which is the resurrection of the
just."[42] and which will be inaugurated by Christ and the
judgement effected by him.[43] This kingdom will come after
six thousand years ("for in the number of days the world was
made, in the same number of thousands of years it is
brought to its consummation"[44]), and the last 'day' of a
thousand years will be a time of rest and sanctification.[45] At
that time Abraham's inheritance (cf. Gen 15:18; 30:2) will be
restored and many will come to the kingdom from east and
west.[46] This kingdom, Irenaeus claims, the Gnostics denied.

> [They] pass over the order of advancement of the just,
> [they] do not accept the salvation of their own flesh ...
> [and they] say that as soon as they are dead they pass over
> the heavens and the Creator and go to their Mother
> [Wisdom].[47]

In the context of the kingdom, Irenaeus brings forward
the raising of Christ in the flesh after three days among the
dead as an example of the need of Christians patiently to
"await the time of our resurrection."[48] This first resurrection

[41]*AH* V.33.4.
[42]*AH* V.33.3.
[43]*AH* V.71. and V.27.1ff.
[44]*AH* V.28.3.
[45]*AH* V.33.2; cf. V.28.3.
[46]*AH* V.33.2.
[47]*AH* V.31.2; cf. V.35.1.
[48]*AH* V.31.2.

brings them to the kingdom which is "the beginning of incorruption."[49] Irenaeus goes on to talk of the abundance and tranquillity of the kingdom,[50] and to quote Old Testaments predictions of it (Isa 26.19; Ezek 37:12-14; 28:25-26; Jer 23.7-8). The healing foretold in Isaiah 30 is the healing of death, "which God shall heal, raising us from the dead and restoring us to the patriarchs' inheritance."[51] The promises clearly "signify the feasting of that creation in the kingdom of the just which God promised that he himsel will minister."[52] Irenaeus warns against interpreting the promises only as allegories: "All these events cannot be understood as happening above the heavens."[53]

> As the human person will truly rise, so will he likewise truly realize incorruption beforehand, and be increased and flourish in the times of the kingdom, that he may be made capable of the glory of the Father.... Since human persons are real, their transformation must be real."[54]

The millenarian kingdom is thus a time of preparation as well, a time of being made "capable of the glory of the Father" which will be manifest when the reign with Christ shall end. At the end of the millenarian kindgom a new and eternal heaven and earth will come. In the absence of any evidence to the contrary, it seems Irenaeus envisaged that the risen bodies would continue in the same manner in that eternal heaven and earth as they had in the millenarian kingdom.

---

[49] *AH* V.32.1.
[50] *AH* V.33.
[51] *AH* V.34.2.
[52] *AH* V.34.3.
[53] *AH* V.35.2.
[54] *AH* V.35.2-36.1.

Tertullian

"The resurrection of the dead is the Christian's confidence. By believing it we are what we claim to be."[55] Tertullian's openly declared motive in refuting the gnostic interpretation was to preserve that confidence and belief. (It has been suggested that his later conversion to Montanism was prompted at least in part by his perception that it was only the Montanists who were defending this and other threatened traditional teachings.[56]) In Tertullian's eyes, as in those of Gnostics, the human reality of Christ's flesh and the possibility of the resurrection of the flesh generally were intimately connected. In his treatise, *On the Flesh of Christ*, he writes.

> [The Gnostics cannot but be apprehensive that,] if it were admitted that [Christ's flesh] was human, this would constitute a leading case against them that flesh certainly does rise again, seeing it has risen again in Christ.... It is his flesh that is under inquisition. Its verity is under discussion, and its quality.... A decision concerning it will lay down the law for our own resurrection.[57]

And in his companion treatise, *On the Resurrection of the Flesh*, he points out again that

> He, who in view of the deposit of both parties entrusted to him is designated joint-trustee of God and men, preserves in himself the deposit of the flesh as an earnest of the whole sum. For just as he has left to us the earnest of the Spirit, so he has received from us the earnest of the flesh and has carried it into heaven as a pledge that the whole

---

[55] *De Resurrectione Carnis* 1. All quotations from this treatise are taken from E.E. Evans, *Tertullian's Treatise on the Resurrection* (London: SPCK, 1960).

[56] J.G. Davies, "Factors leading to the Emergence of Belief in the Resurrection of the Flesh," *JTS* 23 (1972), 651.

[57] *De Carne Christi* 1. All quotations from this treatise are taken from E.E. Evans, *Tertullian's Treatise on the Incarnation* (London: SPCK, 1956).

sum will some day be conveyed thither. Have no fear, flesh and blood: you have already in Christ taken possession of heaven and of the kingdom of God.[58]

The reality of Christ's flesh (against those who denied its existence), its humanness (against those who identified it as a spiritual flesh unique to him) and the possibility of all human flesh being raised were the issues at stake among Christians. Most were agreed on the immortality of the soul[59] (Tertullian himself had already written on that topic), but the teaching of "the modern Sadducees," as Tertullian frequently terms the valentinian Gnostics,[60] was perceived to be the chief threat. He saw their denigration of the flesh and their christological docetism serving their denial of the bodily resurrection (as the passage above shows), and that denial as the necessary premise for their doctrine of two gods.

> [They] begin with the question of the resurrection, because it is harder to believe the resurrection of the flesh than the unity of God. . . . For each several individual, cast down or thrust back from his stance on that hope which he had embraced in the sight of the Creator, thereafter is easily led away, without further suggestion from elsewhere, to surmise the author of another hope.[61]

The valentinian 'invective against the flesh' included attributing a 'spiritual' flesh to Christ. Citing passages from the Old and New Testaments, Tertullian outlines his perception of the root of the gnostic objections to Christ's flesh being the same as that of all other humans, and asserts that it was "not composed of. . . soul or of the stars, nor is it imagi-

---

[58] *RC* 51.
[59] *RC* 1.
[60] *RC* 2.
[61] *RC* 2.

nary."[62] He explains what he understands to be their motives.

> [The Valentinians] refuse to admit that terrestial and human substance was brought into shape for Christ, lest the Lord should turn out to be of less worth than the angels, who do not consist of terrestrial flesh: and secondly, because flesh like ours would have needed to be born like us, not of the Spirit, nor of God, but of the will of a man. "And what," they ask, "is the meaning of 'Not of corruption, but of incorruption?'"[63]

The Gnostics argued that the orthodox Christians held that Christ's flesh was like that of all humans in some respects, but not in others.

> 'And why [they ask], even as that flesh rose again and was received up into heaven, is not ours, if it is like his, straightway taken up? Or else why was not his, if it is like ours, likewise dissolved into the earth?'[64]

Clearly, Tertullian heard the Gnostics response to their own question ("why...is not ours, if it is like his, straightway taken up?") as "because Christ's flesh is not like ours,...for us." One possible reply was, of course, that that promise would be fulfilled in the future. In *On the Resurrection of the Flesh*, Tertullian insists (citing Paul and John) on both the bodily and the future parousial character of the resurrection: "Thus, although in the acknowledgement of the mystery it comes to bud, yet it comes to flower and fruit at the Lord's actual presence."[65]

[62]*CC* 15.
[63]*CC* 15.
[64]*CC* 15.
[65]*CC* 22.
[65]*RC* 22.

By 'body' Tertullian understands 'the fabric of the flesh' and by 'resurrection of the dead' 'resurrection of the flesh,' arguing that since the soul has not fallen the term 'resurrection' cannot properly be applied to it.[66] Tertullian's defence of the flesh of humankind is among the most attractive of his writings. He sees its dignity deriving initially from its creation and salvation by the one God:

> God forbid, that God should abandon to eternal destruction the work of his own hands, the product of his own skill, the receptacle of his own breath, the queen of his own creation, the heir of his generosity, the priest of his cult, the warrior of his testimony, the sister of his Christ.[67]

And in another passage he writes of human flesh as "not only a work of God, but also a token of him," because, in creating it, "the thought was of Christ."[68]

The flesh is the associate of the soul, a servant, not an instrument or a chattel,[69] and therefore shares the responsibilities and the hopes of the soul. Tertullian is concerned to stress the intimacy of the body/soul relationship, not its duality. Did the Valentinians really think, he asks, that God would consign to "some very cheap receptacle the reflection of his own soul, the breath of his own spirit, the workmanship of his own mouth, and would thus by giving it an unworthy lodging definitely bring about its damnation?".[70] Yet God has inserted the soul into the flesh, commingled it with the flesh in so intimate a union that it is difficult to tell whether the body bears the soul, or the soul the body. "[T]he soul," Tertullian decides, "is more akin to God as the rider and master," but it is also to the glory of the flesh that it contain the soul.[71]

[66] *RC* 18.
[67] *RC* 9.
[68] *RC* 6.
[69] *RC* 16.
[70] *RC* 7.
[71] *RC* 7.

> For what enjoyment of nature, what fruition of the
> world, what savouring of the elements, does the soul feed
> upon except by means of the flesh? What think you?
> Through it as intermediary the soul is enriched by the
> whole apparatus of the senses, sight, hearing, taste, smell,
> touch. Through it it is aspersed with divine power, seeing
> it provides for nothing except by speech previously
> expressed, at least in silence: for speech also derives from
> the flesh as its organ. By the flesh are the manual arts, by
> the flesh are liberal and professional studies, by the flesh
> are activities, occupations, and services: and to such a
> degree does the whole of the soul's living belong to the
> flesh, that to the soul to cease to live is exactly the same
> thing as to retire from the flesh. . . . Thus the flesh, while
> it is reckoned the servant and handmaid of the soul, is
> found to be its consort and coheir: if in things temporal,
> why not also in things eternal?[72]

The flesh of the human person, dignified in its creation
and intimately allied to the soul, has with it fallen under the
reign of sin and death.[73] Tertullian points out, in the context
of 'only that can rise which has fallen,' that "by the very fact
that resurrection appertains to a thing liable to fall, namely
flesh, that same flesh will be indicated in the designation
'dead,' because the resurrection which is described as 'of the
dead' is the resurrection of a thing liable to fall."[74] But the
very flesh which has fallen has become sacramental in the
salvific christian dispensation. With an ironical reference to
the gnostic valuation of flesh as 'pitiful and squalid,' Tertullian writes.

> We must next consider also from the private law of the
> Christan nation how great a prerogative this pitiful and
> squalid substance enjoys in the sight of God: though it

[72] *RC* 7.
[73] *RC* 46, 18.
[74] *RC* 18; cf. 12, 28, 34.

would be sufficient for it that no soul can even obtain salvation unless while it is in the flesh it has become a believer. To such a degree is the flesh the pivot of salvation, that since by it the soul becomes linked with God, it is the flesh which makes possible the soul's election by God. For example, the flesh is washed that the soul may be made spotless: the flesh is anointed that the soul may be consecrated: the flesh is signed [with the cross] that the soul too may be protected: the flesh is overshadowed by the imposition of hands that the soul may be illumined by the Spirit: the flesh feeds on the Body and Blood of Christ so that the soul also may be replete with God. There is then no possibility of these, which the work associates, being divided in the wages.[75]

In arguing for the resurrection of the flesh, Tertullian uses most of the themes that had become the stock-in-trade of Christian apologetic, but he uses them hardly more than in passing. Resurrection is well within the divine power: "And certainly he who has made is competent to remake, seeing it is a greater thing to make than to remake, to give a beginning than to give it back again."[76] There is a brief reprise of the analogies found in nature,[77] the phoenix is linked to psalm 92 as found in the Septuagint ("thou shalt flourish like a phoenix"),[78] and "the well-known sublety of vulgar belief"—will not injury and decay prohibit the raising of the body in its integrity?—is dismissed briskly:

> As life is given us by God, so also is it given again: as we were when we received it, so are we also when we receive it back. Our restoration is a gift to nature, not to injury: we live again as we were born, not as what damage makes us.

[75] *RC* 8.
[76] *RC* 11.
[77] *RC* 12.
[78] *RC* 13.

> God is not raising the dead, if he does not raise them entire.[79]

It is, however, on the theme of the justice of the resurrection of the body that Tertullian chiefly bases his argument, in keeping with his understanding of soul and body as so closely entwined.

> [T]hus the plenity and completeness of judgement can be assured only by the production [in court] of the whole man—in fact that the whole man appears in the assemblage of both substances—and consequently he must be made present in both, seeing he needs to be judged as a whole, as assuredly he has not lived except as a whole. Therefore in that state in which he has lived, in that will he be judged, because he has to be judged in respect of his life as he has lived it.[80]

But all these arguments do no more than build the foundation for Tertullian's interpretation of the disputed scriptural passages. The hermeneutical method used to refute the Valentinians' spiritual understanding of the resurrection is explicitly stated:

> And, indeed, [since some passages are more obscure than others], it would be equitable...that things uncertain should be prejudged by things certain, and things obscure by things manifest, at the least so that between the disagreement of things certain and things uncertain, of things manifest and things obscure, faith should not be frittered away, truth brought into danger, and God himself stigmatized as inconstant.[81]

---

[79] *RC* 57.
[80] *RC* 14; cf. 34.
[81] *RC* 21.

In this same passge Tertullian urges the necessity of the certainty of the resurrection of the flesh for the spread of the Christian faith.

> [I]t is not likely that that aspect of the mystery to which the whole faith is entrusted, on which the whole discipline is supported, should turn out to have been ambiguously announced and obscurely propounded, when the hope of the resurrection, unless it were manifest in respect of peril and reward, would persuade no one to a religion, particularly of this kind, which is the object of public hatred and hostile accusation. No work is certain, of which the wages are uncertain: no fear is well-founded, of a peril which is in doubt. Yet both the wages and the peril depend on the issue of the resurrection.[82]

Reference was made earlier to the gnostic interpretation of Paul, and it is with a lengthy counter-exegesis, not only of Paul, but of the Scriptures generally, that Tertullian concludes his argument:

> [W]e must pay attention to those scriptures also which forbid us, after the manner of these soulful men—let me not call them spiritual—either to assume that the resurrection is already present in the acknowledgement of the truth, or to claim that it ensues immediately upon departure from this life.[83]

Paul, the Apocalypse, even the prophets of the Old Testament plainly teach the futurity of the resurrection.[84] Christ's words in the gospels are appealed to on the basis of the hermeneutical principle outlined earlier.

> If the names of the things, that is, 'judgement' and 'king-

[82] *RC* 21; cf. 33.
[83] *RC* 22.
[84] *RC* 23-32.

> dom of God' and 'resurrection' have an evident meaning,
> so that nothing of theirs can be constrained into a para-
> ble, neither can those things be forced into parables
> which are preached respecting the establishment, the
> administration, the downfall, and the resurrection of the
> Jewish kingdom: and thus they will establish their claim
> to be corporal, as being destined for corporal beings, and
> in that case not spiritual, because not metaphorical.[85]

Tertullian then moves on to exegete the pauline texts to
counter the gnostic interpretation, beginning with 2 Corinthians 4:16—"although our outward man is decaying, yet
our inward man is being renewed from day to day." The
Gnostics read it as the destruction of the body and the
salvation of the soul, the substance of the human. But 'man,'
Tertullian explains, means body and soul, the 'inward man'
does not mean the substance, but the 'flavour' or disposition
of the person. While the 'outward man' is "worn away by
afflictions and injuries," the 'inward man' is renewed by
"faith and doctrine day by day, now, not hereafter."[86]
Returning to his favourite theme that the soul and body are
allied in trial and reward, Tertullian assures his readers that

> Although the outward man is decaying, it is understood
> to be decaying not as being deprived of resurrection but
> as suffering vexation, and that not apart from the inner
> man. So it will appertain to both to be glorified together
> just as it does to suffer together: for association in profits
> must of necessity run in accordance with partnership in
> toil.[87]

The heavenly profit is the incorruption promised in 1 Corinthians 15:51-53, but it does not involve the destruction of the
body.

[85] *RC* 33.
[86] *RC* 40.
[87] *RC* 40.

For when [Paul] adds, "This corruptible thing must put on incorruption, and this mortal thing must put on immortality," this will be that dwelling-place from heaven with which, while groaning in the flesh, we desire to be clothed upon, surely 'upon' the flesh in which we shall be found: because he says we who are in the tabernacle are burdened because we would not be unclothed but rather clothed upon, that the mortal thing may be swallowed up of life, evidently while it is being changed by being clothed upon with that which is from heaven.[88]

'Overgarment of immortality' and 'being clothed upon' become Tertullian's favourite, almost exlusive, way of describing the resurrection body.[89] The image is one of a glorious and all-enveloping outer robe, but one which precisely is an outer robe and requires an inner garment: "To be clothed upon can evidently only apply to one who is already dressed."[90] This concept is combined, with that of the seed to which God will give a body pleasing to him, in this passage:

To what purpose then will God give it a body according as he wishes, when it has all the time that naked body which is its own, unless with the intention of its rising again not naked. Consequently there will be an additional body, which is built over the body, and that over which it is built up is not abolished but increased. But a thing that is increased is conserved. For when sown it is merely grain without the clothing of its husk... But when it rises up it has made interest by multiplication.... It has from God another body which...is changed not by destruction but by enlargement.[91]

[88] *RC* 42.
[89] *RC* 42.
[90] *RC* 42.
[91] *RC* 52.

The Gnostics read 2 Corinthians 4:10-11—"always carrying in the body the death of Jesus, so that the life of Jesus may also be manifested in our bodies for while we live we are always being given up to death for Jesus' sake, so that the life of Jesus may be manifested in our mortal flesh"—as an injunction to holiness in this life: "The life of Jesus has now to be manifested in our body by means of the discipline of holiness and patience and righteousness and wisdom. . . ."[92] Tertullian, however, insists on its future reference.

> Thus he means that this will come to pass in our body after we are dead. But if then, how, unless it has been raised again? Accordingly he also says, at the conclusion, "Knowing that he who hath raised up Jesus will also raise us up along with him," because he has already risen again from the dead: unless it is that "along with him" means "like him." But if it means "like him," then certainly not without flesh.[93]

And then what Tertullian sees as "the final assault," the interpretation of the text upon which the Gnostics "built up at the very first onset,"[94] that is, 1 Corinthians 15:50—"flesh and blood cannot inherit the kingdom of God." "Under what conditions the apostle has disinherited these substances from the kingdom of God" can be learned from the context, Tertullian says.[95] Here, as consistently throughout the treatise, his point is that Paul's apparent injunctions agains the flesh are really injunctions against sin.[96] Discussing the first and the last Adam text, he writes:

> We have worn the image of the earthly man by partnership in transgression, by fellowship in death, by exile

[92] *RC* 44.
[93] *RC* 44.
[94] *RC* 44.
[94] *RC* 48.
[95] *RC* 49.
[96] Cf. *RC* 45, 46, 49, 50.

from paradise. For though it is in the flesh that here the image of Adam is worn, yet it is not the flesh we are enjoined to take off: and if not the flesh, then it is the life and manners, so that we may thereby also wear in us the image of the heavenly, though we are not yet gods, not yet established in heaven, but according to the lineaments of Christ are proceeding in holiness and righteousness and truth.... Since therefore he makes the image of the earthly and of the heavenly a matter of life and manners, the former to be forsworn, the latter to be sought after,.. he requires us to understand by "flesh and blood" no other thing than the previously mentioned "image of the man": and if this image has its origin in our "former conversation," and the former conversation is incapable of the kingdom of God, it follows that flesh and blood, as not being capable of the kingdom of God, are reduced to "former conversation."[97]

Moral conduct will be judged after the resurrection.

For it is not resurrection which is in set terms denied to flesh and blood, but the kingdom of God, which is a concomitant of the resurrection, though there is also a resurrection unto judgement: rather, a general resurrection of the flesh is even confirmed by the very fact a specific one is excepted. For while announcement is made into what state it does not rise again, one tacitly understands into what state it does rise again. And thus, while the work of the substance, not its genus, experiences in accordance with its merits a distinction in resurrection, it is evident from this besides that flesh and blood are kept out of the kingdom of God on account of guilt, not of substance.... And so all flesh and blood, without distinction, do rise again in their proper quality; but those to whom it appertains to approach to the kingdom of God will, before they are able to obtain it, have to clothe themselves with that principle of incorruptibility and immortality without which they cannot approach to the kingdom of God.[98]

The point of reference, as always, is Christ.

Then how did Christ rise again? In the flesh, or not? Undoubtedly if you hear that he died, that he was buried, according to the scriptures, and not otherwise than in the flesh, you must no less admit that he was raised again in the flesh: for that very thing which died in death, which lay down in burial, this it is which has also risen again, not so much Christ in the flesh as the flesh in Christ. Therefore if we are to rise again after Christ's example, and he rose again in the flesh—well, we shall not be rising again after Christ's example if we are not ourselves also to rise again in the flesh.[99]

To clinch his argument, Tertullian asks why Paul would have been so concerned about the nature of the resurrection body if the body were not to be raised: "The resurrection is defined as corporal, since it is with the quality of bodies that the discussion is concerned."[100] Tertullian frequently states that the resurrection body, with its 'overgarment' will be like that of the angels, meaning, he explains, "no more tied to the usages of the flesh."[101] The present body will be changed, not destroyed. Although one might think a body useless in the kingdom of God where none of the circumstances which require a body will obtain, Tertullian insists that

You will have no right, on the ground that the member will in the future be inactive, to deny the possibility of its existing anew: for it is feasible for a thing to exist anew

[98] *RC* 50.
[99] *RC* 48.
[100] *RC* 48.
[101] *RC* 62.

and none the less be inactive. But it cannot be said even to be inactive, if it does not exist. Moreover, if it exist, it will be possible for it also not to be inactive: for in God's presence nothing can be inactive.[102]

Describing the resurrection body, Tertullian writes of flesh free from "every harassing malady,"[103] "the same in essence, only more full and more perfect," the flesh of this life receiving in itself "the grace and ornament which God shall please to spread over it, according to its merits."[104] Recalling Paul's nuptial imagery, he concludes:

> So then the flesh will rise again, all of it indeed, itself, entire. Wherever it is, it is on deposit with God through the faithful trustee of God and men, Jesus Christ, who will pay back both God to man and man to God, spirit to flesh and flesh to spirit. He has already made the alliance of both in himself, brought the bride to the bridegroom and the bridegroom to the bride. For even if one shall claim that the soul is the bride, the flesh will go with the soul, at least in the name of dowry: the soul must be no prostitute, to be taken up by the bridegroom without assets. She has her chattels, her raiment, her serving-maid, the flesh: it will accompany her as a foster-sister. But it is the flesh which is the bride, for in Christ Jesus it has taken the Spirit as bridegroom by means of blood.[105]

[102] *RC* 60.
[103] *RC* 61; cf. 57.
[104] *RC* 52.
[105] *RC* 63.

5. CLEMENT, ORIGEN AND METHODIUS

Clement of Alexandria

The confrontational polemic of Irenaeus and Tertullian was not the only reaction to Gnosticism, nor was *The Epistle to Rheginos* the only attempt to find a middle ground between the extremes of opinion of the materialists and of those who denied the resurrection altogether. There is a sense in which the 'gnostic' is as much a personality type as a believer in a particular doctrine, and it was for such persons within orthodox Christianity that the mediators wrote (on the resurrection as on other topics) in an attempt to meet the Gnostics on their own ground. Clement of Alexandria—to take one well known example—shared with the Gnostics the conviction that knowledge of God was the highest human happiness and destiny, and his writings argue the case for a christian Gnosticism. However, the more one's view of the afterlife envisages it as intellectual, the harder it is to account for the presence of the body there. The treatise Clement wrote on the resurrection is lost, and the teaching on the subject which can be pieced together from his other writings leaves certain questions—notably his understanding of the resurrection body—unanswered, or answered only partially.

Clement teaches that Adam's sin was lack of docility; he refused to pay heed to God's command.

> [Adam] fell victim to pleasure... and he was led astray by his desires, the child becoming adult through disobedience and, refusing to listen to the Father, he was ashamed before God.[1]

Although it is not a point that he labours, Clement identifies this sin as the cause of human mortality and Christ's death as that which makes human immortality possible.

> [Christ is] the Word of truth, the Word of incorruption, who regenerates the human person by raising him to the truth. He is the spur of salvation, who banishes corruption and expels death.[2]

Despite Adam's sin, the human person is given at creation the image of God—the intellect—, the image which is never completely erased by personal sin. It is the source of the ineradicable yearning for God which causes some, at least, to allow themselves to be educated to contemplation and immortality, the diametrical opposite of the eternal death of sin.

Clement's soteriology, which owes much (as did his theology generally) to platonic philosophy and allegorical interpretation in the tradition of Philo, reflects this view of sin and death, and is thus one of, first, forgiveness of sins in baptism,[3] and, following that, of education to bring one to God.

> [T]hrough [Christ] all men belong to him, but some by way of knowledge, while others have not yet attained to this; some as faithful servants, others as servants merely.

[1] *Prot.* XI.111.1.
[2] *Prot.* XI.117.4.
[3] *Paed.* I.vi.26.

> This is the Teacher who educates the gnostic by means
> of mysteries, and the believer by means of good hopes,
> and him who is hard of heart by means of corrective
> discipline acting on the senses.[4]

Human sin, in Clement's view, is entirely an act of the free
will, it "is an activity, not an existence,"[5] and so Christ's life
is presented in an exemplary and paedagogical context, and
his death as a redemption[6] of humankind from the corruption which results from sin.

> The Lord wished to deliver man from his bonds. [Him-
> self] bound in flesh (a divine mystery), he overcame the
> serpent and reduced the tyrant to servitude. What is even
> more surprising, that same man, led astray by pleasure
> and corruption, was shown to be free again by [Christ's]
> outstretched arms.[7]

In Clement's thought, however, the delivery effected by
Christ's death is a preliminary to the attainment of that true
gnosis where Christ is light, truth and life. The groundwork
of this state is laid by the discipline of a virtuous life. Adam,
he writes, was not created perfect (if he had been, would he
have sinned?), but 'apt for virtue' and all his descendants are
similarly constituted.

> [I]n regard to virtue, it is very important to be made fit for
> its attainment. And it is intended that we should be saved
> by ourselves.... [W]e are rational and, philosophy being
> rational, we have some aptitude for it.... But one man
> applies less, one more, to learning and training. Where-
> fore also some have been competent to attain to perfect

---

[4]*Strom.* VII.ii.5-6; Cf. IV.v.19. All quotations from books 3 and 7 of the
Stromata are taken from J.E.L Oulton and H. Chadwick, *Alexandrian Christianity* (London: SCM, 1954).

[5]*Strom.* IV.xiii.94; cf. V. xiv.90.

[6]*Paed.* I.v.23.

[7]*Prot.* XI.111.2.

virtue, and others have attained to a kind of it. And some, on the other hand, through negligence, although in other respects of good disposition, have turned to the opposite. Now that knowledge which excels all branches of culture in importance and truth is much more difficult to acquire, and is attained with great effort.[8]

The *Stromata* has several depictions of the 'good gnostic' who is pious, obedient to the commandments, "restraining pleasure and desire, grief and anger, and, in general, [able] to resist anything which either by force or fraud entices."[9] He or she is a student of philosophy which "purges the soul and prepares it before hand for the reception of faith, on which the Truth builds up the edifice of knowledge."[10] The Eucharist, in Clement's theology, is the food of incorruptibility. Quoting John 6:51 ("The bread which I will give is my flesh for the life of the world"), he writes:

> One must note here the mystical sense of 'bread.'[Christ] says that it is his flesh, certainly his risen flesh. As the wheat which springs from decomposition and sowing, so is his flesh reconstituted, after the trial of fire, to the joy of the church. It is like the bread which has been baked. Since he said 'the bread which I will give is my flesh' and because, as well, blood flows through flesh, and because wine, taken allegorically, means blood, it must be understood thus: when morsels of bread are added to adulterated wine, the bread aborbs the wine and leaves only that which is watery. In the same way, the flesh of the Lord, the bread of heaven, absorbs the blood [of human persons], raising those who are heavenly to incorruptibility,

[8]*Strom.* VI.xii.96. All quotations from the other books of the *Stromata* are taken from W. Wilson, *The Writings of Clement of Alexandria* (Edinburgh: T. and T. Clarke, 1971), 2 vols., slightly altered.

[9]*Strom.* VII.iii.17.

[10]*Strom.* VII.iii.20.

> and leaves only the carnal desires destined for corruption.[11]

Although the stress in Clement's works in on the knowledge of God and the means of attaining that knowledge, he was not a docetist in his christology. We read in the *Stromata* that

> The Saviour... could never be a hater of the human race for it was owing to his abounding love... that he did not scorn the weakness of human flesh, but, having clothed himself with it, came into the world for common human salvation.[12]

And again he writes:

> Without the body how could the divine plan for us in the church achieve its end? Surely the Lord himself, the Head of the church, came in the flesh...to teach us to look upon the formless and incorporeal nature of the divine Cause.[13]

Nor does he think the human body evil. Writing in refutation of the Gnostics who "vilify the body" he argues that

> The soul of man is confessedly the better part and the body the inferior. But neither is the soul good by nature, nor, on the other hand, is the body by nature bad. Nor is that which is not good entirely bad. For there are things which occupy a middle place, and among them are things to be preferred and things to be rejected. The constitution of man, then, which has its place among the things of sense, was necessarily composed of things different, but not opposed—body and soul.[14]

[11] *Paed.* I.vi.46-47.
[12] *Strom.* VII.ii.8.
[13] *Strom.* III.xvii.103.3.
[14] *Strom.* IV.xxvi.164.3-5.

and also:

> Does not the Saviour who heals the soul also heal the body of its passions? But if the flesh were hostile to the soul, he would not have raised an obstacle to the soul by strengthening the hostile flesh with good health.[15]

Nevertheless, the human goal is to rise above the flesh, as the example of Christ teaches.

> He is then properly called the Teacher of the beings formed by him. Nor does he even abandon care for men, . . . he who, having assumed flesh, which by nature is susceptible of suffering, trained it to the condition of impassibility.[16]

And elsewhere Clement writes that "[Philip] rose from the tomb when the Lord killed his passions, and he began to live unto Christ."[17]

This present resurrection in knowledge is a foretaste of the eternal,[18] and, Clement teaches that, the human person is indeed created for immortality.

> 'For God created man for immortality, and made him an image of his own nature' (Wis 2:22), according to which nature of [God] who knows all, he who is a gnostic, and, righteous and holy with prudence, hastens to reach the measure of perfect manhood.[19]

He envisages a hierarchy of happiness in the afterlife, taking the ranks from the offices of the church (apostles, bishops, priests and deacons).

[15]*Strom.* III. . .
[16]*Strom.* VII.ii.7.
[17]*Strom.* III.iv.25.
[18]*Paed.* I.vi.29.
[19]*Strom.* VI.xii.97.

> [T]here are various abodes, according to the worth of
> those who have believed...for there are lower parts in
> the temple of God, which is the whole church.[20] The
> grades here in the church are imitations of the angelic
> glory and of that economy which...awaits those
> who...have lived in perfection of righteousness accord-
> ing to the gospel."[21]

The criterion for that hierarchy will be knowledge:

> And the chosen of the chosen are those who by reason of
> perfect knowledge are culled from the church itself, and
> honoured with the most august glory....[22]

It is against the background of this highly intellectual
understanding of the afterlife that one should assess the
place Clement assigned in it to the body, but there is not
enough information to do so accurately. He affirmed the
resurrection of the body several times. There are two allusions to it in *The Tutor*, one in the context of psalm 1:3,
where the "leaf which does not fall off" is taken as a reference to the body, and another in that of psalm 150:4, where
"praise him with tambour and choir" is interpreted as "the
church, hearing the skin of the tambourine resonate, [so]
thinks of the resurrection of the body."[23] But the nature of
that body is unclear. Clement taught that sexual differenta-
tion will disappear: men [*andrasin*] and women [*gynaizin*]
will be 'human' [*anthropos*], but the question whether this
will be a change in the body, or a change in attitude, arises
when we read that this state will be a result of liberation
"from the desire which separates them here."[24]

Despite his positive attitude towards the body (cf. especially Book 3 of the *Stromata*), Clement's primary interest

[20]*Strom. VI.xiv.114.1-2.*
[21]*Strom.* VI.xiii.107.2.
[22]*Strom.* vi.xiii.107.2.
[23]*Paed.* II. iv.41.
[24]*Paed.* I.iv.10.

and emphasis lay not in its fate, but in the perfection of the knowledge of faith. He asserts in the *Tutor* that baptism and the gift of the Spirit brings one into the light, even if the perfect gift has not yet been received. This conviction that the joy of heaven will be nothing of a different order, but the perfection of the wisdom of this life was a very important one to him.

> [The fullness of light] is reserved until the resurrection of those who believe; and it is does not consist in receiving any new good, but only in taking possession of that which was promised earlier. For we do not say that both [the promise and the fulfilment] take place together and at the same time.... For eternity and time are not the same thing, neither is the attempt and the final result; but both refer to the same thing, and one and the same person is concerned in both. Faith, so to speak, is the attempt generated in time; the final result is the secure attainment of the promise for eternity.... If then, those who have believed have everlasting life [Jn 3:36], what more is there beyond the possession of everlasting life?... Where faith is, there the promise is, and the consummation of the promise is rest, our final goal. After our departure from this life, there is not a different sort of thing awaiting us who have believed here below, and who have received a pledge for all time. That future good which we have already grasped in faith, we shall, after the resurrection, seize it as a good attained.[25]

And again in the *Stromata*:

> Knowledge, therefore, is swift to purify and suitable for the welcome change to the higher state. Hence, too, it easily transplants a person to that divine and holy state which is akin to the soul, and by a light of its own carries him through the mystic stages, till it restores him to the

[25] *Paed.* I.vi.28-29,

crowning abode of rest, having taught the pure in heart to look upon God face to face with understanding and absolute certainty. For herein lies the perfection of the gnostic soul, that having transcended all purifications and modes of ritual, it should be with the Lord where he is, in immediate subordination to him.[26]

Origen

In Origen we meet one of the most important theologians of the patristic age (only Augustine is comparable) and one who has throughout the centuries both attracted keen admirers and touched off lasting controversies. His teaching on the resurrection aroused bitter opposition from certain Christians from the late third century on. Origen was not the first to stress the spiritual nature of the resurrection body (as has been seen), but his stature, the vigour with which he did so and the barely concealed contempt for those who taught the revivification of the material body brought a new dimension to the discussion. Some of the teachings on the resurrection attributed to Origen were condemned in the sixth century.[27] There is the usual discussion concerning the similarity between what was condemned and what Origen actually taught, and ascertaining that teaching is complicated by the suspicion of a benevolence on the part of his admirer and translator, Rufinus, which may have modified some of Origen's more adventuresome speculations.[28]

Origen was traditional in teaching the twofold death of the Christian—that of the body, the result of Adam's sin[29]

[26]*Strom.* VII.x.56-57.

[27]Cf. H. Denzinger, *Enchiridion Symbolorum* [editio 31] (Herder: Freiburg im B., 1957), 3207. The curious accusation that Origen taught that the resurrection body would be spherical ('orbiculata') has been discussed by H. Chadwick, "Origen, Celsus, and the Resurrection of the Body," *Harvard Theological Review* 41 (1948) 83-102.

[28]Cf. J.N.D. Kelly, *Jerome, his Life, Writings, and Controversies* (New York: Harper and Row, 1974), 227-34.

[29]*Hom.Ez.* 1.9; *Hom.Jer.* 2.1.

and that of the soul, the result of personal sin. In the *Dialogue with Heraclides* he discusses the mortality and immortality of the soul. Responding to a question from bishop Demetrius, Origen explains.

The remark of father Demetrius has given us the starting point for another problem. He asserted that we have said the soul is immortal. To this I will say that the soul is immortal and the soul is not immortal. Let us first define the meaning of the word 'death' and determine all its possible senses. I will try to show all its meanings...as found in the divine Scripture. Perhaps one more learned than I will point out other senses also. But for the present I am aware of three kinds of death. What are these three kinds of death? According to the apostle, a man may live unto God and die unto sin. This death is a blessed thing. A man dies to sin. This death my Lord died. "For in that he died, he died unto sin." I know also another sort of death, according to which a man dies to God; concerning this it was said: "The soul that sins, it shall die." And I know a third kind of death, according to which we commonly suppose that those who are separated from the body die. For "Adam" lived nine hundred and thirty years and died."

There being, then, three kinds of death, let us see whether the human soul is immortal in respect of the three kinds of death, or if not in respect of the three, yet in respect of some of them. The death that is a matter of moral indifference all men die. It is that which we consider dissolution. No soul of man dies this death. For it it did so, it would not be punished after death. It is said: "Men shall seek for death and shall not find it." In this sense every human soul is immortal. But in the other meanings, the soul in the one sense is mortal, and blessed if it dies to sin. It is of this death that Balaam spoke when he prophesied, praying by divine inspiration: "May my soul die among the souls of the just." Concerning this death Balaam made his astonishing prophecy, and by the word of God he mad for himself a splendid prayer. For he prayed that he might die to sin that he might live unto

God. And this account he said: "May my soul die among the souls of the just and my posterity be like their posterity." There is another death in respect of which we are not immortal, although we have power by exercising vigilance to avoid death. And perhaps that which is mortal in the soul is not for ever mortal. For in so far as it gives way to sin, so that the word is realized which says, "the soul that sins, it shall die," the soul is mortal and dies a real death. But it it is found firmly established in blessedness so that it is inaccessible to death, because it has eternal life, it is not longer mortal but in this sense has even become immortal.[30]

It has been said that salvation history, for Origen, "could be understood in terms of the loss and restoration of relative immortality."[31]

The general context of Origen's anthropology is the confinement, not to say punishment, which he understood the existence of the human soul in the body to be. His doctrine of the pre-existence and descent of human souls is well-known; we read, for instance that

When rational souls reach the neighbourhood of the earth they are enclosed in grosser bodies and last of all tied to human flesh.[32]

One might, therefore, expect that salvation for Origen would involve the sloughing-off of the body entirely, as the Gnostics were accused of teaching, but he argues strongly against this position. In *On First Principles* he writes that he

---

[30]*Dialogue to Heraclides*, 25-76 Translation by H. Chadwick taken from *Alexandrian Christianity*. London: SCM, 1954, JEL Oulton & H. Chadwick, eds. 453-454.

[31]L.R. Hennessey, "Origen of Alexandria: the fate of the soul and body after death," unpublished paper.

[32]*De Principiis* I.iv.1. All quotations from *On First Principles* are taken from G.W. Butterworth, trans. *Origen: On First Principles* (New York: Harper and Row, 1966).

has difficulty with the ideas of those who say that the material world will at the eschaton utterly perish.

> We ask therefore in what sense those [things] that are 'seen' are 'temporal'? Does it mean that in all those periods and ages to come, in which the dispersion and division of the one beginning is the to be restored to one and the same end and likeness, there will exist nothing whatever corresponding to this present world? Or is it rather that while the form of the things that are 'seen' passes away, their substance is by no means destroyed? Now Paul seems to confirm the latter explanation when he says, "the form of this world shall pass away".... If "the form of this world passes away" it is not by any means an annihilation or destruction of the material substance that is indicated, but the occurrence of a certain change of quality and an alteration of the outward form.
>
> Isaiah too, when he says in prophecy that "there shall be a new heaven and a new earth" undoubtedly suggests a similar thought. For the renewal of "heaven and earth" and the transformation of the "form of this world" and the alteration of the "heavens" will undoubtedly be accomplished in readiness for those who are journeying along the way which we have indicated above [a reference to Origen's doctrine of progressive purification], making for that end, namely, blessedness, to which we are told that even God's enemies themselves are to be subjected, the end in which God is said to be "all" and "in all." And if anyone thinks that in this "end" material or bodily nature will utterly perish, he can provide no answer whatever to my difficulty, how beings so numerous and mighty can exist and live their life without bodies; since we believe that to exist without material substance and apart from any association with a bodily element is a thing that belongs only to the nature of God. Perhaps somebody else will say that in the end every bodily substance will be so pure and refined that we must think of it as being like the other, as it were of a heavenly purity and clearness. But exactly how it will be is known to God alone and to

those who through Christ and the Holy Spirit are the "friends" of God.[33]

The suggestion of the purified and bodies is, of course, Origen's own.

Those who denied the resurrection of the body could have been Pagans or Gnostics, but it was probably against the latter that Origen is writing, in the work just cited. Some thought that christian beliefs about the resurrection of the body were "foolish and silly." Origen meets them with arguments from scripture and stresses the pauline 'spiritual body':

> The chief objectors are the heretics, who must, I think, be answered in the following manner. If they admit with us that there is a resurrection, let them answer this question: "what was it that died? Was it not a body?" If so, there will be a resurrection of the body. Then again, let them say whether they believe that we are to possess bodies, or not. I submit that, seeing that the apostle Paul says, "It is sown a natural body, it will rise again a spiritual body," these men cannot deny that a body rises or that in the resurrection we are to possess bodies, and if those bodies which have fallen are declared to rise again—and the expression "rise again" could not properly be used except of that which had previously fallen—then no one can doubt that these bodies rise again in order that at the resurrection we may once more be clothed with them. For if bodies rise again, undoubtedly they rise again as a clothing for us, and if it is necessary, as it certainly is, for us to live in bodies, we ought to live in no other bodies but our own. And if it is true that they rise again and do so as "spiritual," there is no doubt that this means that they rise again from the dead with corruption banished and mortality laid aside; otherwise it would seem vain and useless for a man to rise from the dead in order to die over again. Finally, this can be the more clearly understood by care-

[33] *Princ.* I.vi.4.

fully observing what is the quality of the "natural body" which, when sown in the earth, can reproduce the quality of a "spiritual body." For it is from the natural body that the very power and grace of the resurrection evokes the spiritual body, when it transforms it from dishonour to glory.[34]

The transformation from dishonour to glory is from corruptibility to incorruptibility. Again in *On First Principles* Origen writes that

This matter of the body...which now is corruptible, shall put on incorruption when a perfect soul, instructed in the doctrines of incorruption, has begun to use it.[35]

He continues

And I would not have you be surprised that we should use the metaphor of bodily clothing to describe a perfect soul, which on account of the word of God and his wisdom is here called 'incorruption.' For indeed Jesus Christ himself, who is the Lord and Creator of the soul, is said to be the 'clothing' of the saints (Rom 13:14)....As therefore, Christ is the clothing of the soul, so by an intelligible kind of reasoning the soul is said to be the clothing of the body; for it is an ornament of the body, covering and concealing its mortal nature.... [The Apostle means to say], "This body, with its corruptible nature, must receive the clothing of incorruption," that is, a soul that possesses itself in incorruption, by virtue of the fact that it has put on Christ.... And when this body, which one day we will possess in a more glorious form, shall have become a partaker of life, it will then in addition to being immortal, become also incorruptible. For whatever is mortal is on that account corruptible,

[34] *Princ.* II.x.1.
[35] *Princ.* II.iii.2.

but we cannot say that what is corruptible is also mortal [unless it has lived].[36]

The idea of the spiritual body being 'evoked' from the natural body (cf. above, p. 127) is another way of expressing Origen's favourite 'seed' metaphor.

> This change...we must certainly look forward to, and we are undoubtedly right in expecting it to consist in some act that is worthy of the divine grace; for we believe that it will be a change of like character to that in which, as the apostle describes it, a "bare grain of wheat or of some other kind" is sown in the earth, but "God giveth it a body as it pleased him," after the grain of wheat itself has first died.
>
> So we must suppose that our bodies, like a grain of corn, fall into the earth, but that implanted in them is the life-principle which contains the essence of the body: and although the bodies die and are corrupted and scattered, nevertheless by the word of God that same life principle which has all along been preserved in the essence of the body raises them up from the earth and restores and refashions them.[37]

And a fragment from his commentary on Isaiah reads:

> It is better...to say that we shall all rise again. Even the wicked will come to that place where is weeping and gnashing of teeth and where the righteous shall each in his order, receive reward according to the merit of his good deeds. Then the body of their humiliation shall be transformed so as to become like to the glory of the body of Christ.[38]

---

[36] *Princ.* II.iii.2.

[37] *Princ.* II.x.3.

[38] *On Isaiah*, fragment. All quotations from the fragment on Isaiah and the commentaries on the psalms are taken from R.B. Tollinton, trans. *Selections from the Commentaries and Homilies of Origen* (London: SPCK, 1929).

The nature of the risen body will depend on the merit of the individual, Origen teaches.

> In the case of those who shall be counted worthy of obtaining an inheritance in the kingdom of the heavens, the life principle before mentioned, by which the body is refashioned, as the command of God refashions out of the earthly and natural body a spiritual body, which can dwell in the heavens; while to those who have proved of inferior merit, or of something still meaner than this, or even of the lowest and most insignificant grade, will be given a body of glory and dignity corresponding to the dignity of each one's life and soul; in such a way, however, that even for those who are to be destined to "eternal fire" or to "punishments" the body that rises is so incorruptible, through the transformation wrought by the resurrection, that it cannot be corrupted and dissolved even by punishments.[39]

And in reference to Rev 20:6 ("Over such [those who share in the first resurrection] death has no power, but they shall be priests of God and of Christ, and they shall reign with him for a thousand years") Origen avoids the millenarian interpretation, and interprets the idea of two resurrections in the following way:

> It is right...to enquire whether perhaps the whole scheme of the resurrection ought not to be divided into two portions; one, that is, of those who are to be saved, the righteous, the other of those who are to be punished, the sinners.... The one is in all respects pure, joyous, full of all gladness. The other is altogether wretched, altogether full of sadness, appropriate to the deeds and life of men who in this present existence have despised God's commandments and, putting aside all fear of his

[39] *Princ.* II.x.3.

judgment, have given themselves over to the working of all uncleanness and covetousness.[40]

In *On First Principles* he raises the question of the ultimate salvation of all:

> But I think that, from among those that have been made subject to the worse kind of rulers and authorities and world powers, in each world or in certain worlds, there are some who, by reason of their good deeds and their desire to be transferred from these powers will speedily attain manhood by reason of the power of free-will which is in them, or whether it be true that long-continued and deep-rooted wickedness turns at last from a habit into a kind of nature, you, reader, must judge; whether, that is, this portion of the creation shall be utterly and entirely out of harmony even with that final unity and concord, both in the ages that are 'seen' and 'temporal' and in those that are 'not seen' and 'eternal,' all those beings are arranged in a definite order proportionate to the degree and excellence of their merits. And so it happens that some in the first, others in the second, and others even in the last times, through their endurance of greater and more severe punishments of long duration, extending, if I may say so, over many ages, are by these very stern methods of correction renewed and restored, first by the instruction of angels and afterwards by that of powers yet higher in rank, so that they advance through each grade to a higher one, until at length they reach the things that are 'invisible' and 'eternal,' having traversed in turn, by some form of instruction, every single office of the heavenly powers.[41]

Although the decision is left to the reader, it is well known that Origen thought none would be damned eternally:

[40]*Isa. fragment.*
[41]*Princ.*I.vi.3.

> There is a resurrection of the dead, and there is punishment, but not everlasting. For when the body is punished the soul is gradually purified, and so is restored to its ancient rank. ... For all wicked men, and for daemons, too, punishment has an end, and both wicked men and daemons shall be restored to their former rank.[42]

Origen's concern was not only with those who denied the resurrection of the body or the immortality of the soul, but also with those within the church who understood the resurrection in what he considered to be an excessively materialistic way. It will be recalled that he considered such a resurrection unworthy of God (cf. above, p. 128) and he assures the pagan, Celsus, that such is not indeed christian belief:

> Neither we nor the divine scriptures maintain that those long dead will rise up from the earth and live in the same bodies without undergoing any change for the better; and in saying this Celsus falsely accuses us. For we also hear many scriptures that speak of the resurrection in a way worthy of God [Origen here quotes 1 Cor 15.35-38] .... Therefore our hope is not one of *worms*, nor does our soul *desire a body that has rotted.*[43]

Resurrection "in a way worthy of God" is a resurrection that abolishes for ever death and sin, and therefore could not, in Origen's eyes, be the raising of a material body. And, in any case, he argueds the essence of the human lies elsewhere.

> The soul that has studied wisdom...understands the difference between the earthly house which is destroyed, in which is the tabernacle, and the tabernacle itself, in

[42]*Princ.* II.x.8.

[43]*Contra Celsum* V.18. All quotations from *Against Celsus* are taken from H. Chadwick, *Origen: Contra Celsum* (Cambridge: Cambridge University Press, 1953), p. 277.

which those who are righteous groan being burdened, not
because they desire to put off the tabernacle, but because
they want to be clothed upon, in order that, as a result of
this, "mortality may be swallowed up by life." For since
the nature of the body is to be entirely corruptible, this
mortal tabernacle must put on incorruptibility, and its
other part, which is mortal and capable of death which is
the consequence of sin, must put on immortality; so that
when corruptibility shall put on incorruptibility and mortality immortality then shall come to pass what was foretold long ago by the prophets, the destruction of death's
victory.[44]

Yet it is clear thar, despite the cogency of his arguments,
Origen's understanding of the resurrection was not the only
one, probably not the prevailing one, in the church of the
mid-third century. In *On First Principles* he describes:

Some of our own people, who either from poverty of
intellect or from lack of instruction introduce an exceed-
ingly low and mean idea of the rest of the body....
Certainly if they believe the apostle, who says that the
body, when it rises in glory and in power and in incorruptibility, has already become spiritual, it seems absurd and
contrary to his meaning to say that it is still entangled in
the passions of flesh and blood.[45]

And his exasperation in trying to discuss the matter with his
fellow Christians is apparent in the following passage from
his commentaries on the psalms:

'Therefore the wicked shall not rise up in judgment'
[Ps.1.5]. Prompted by this passage the simpler sort of
believers hold that the wicked will have no share in the
resurrection, though they by no means make it clear what
they understand by the resurrection, or what sort of idea

[44]*Celsus*, V.19.
[45]*Princ.* II.x.3.

they have of the judgment.... Thus if we ask them of what part of them it is that a resurrection takes place, they answer that it is of the bodies wherewith at present we are clothed. Then, on our further asking whether it is of the whole of their substance or not, they say without consideration, "yes, of the whole." But if...we put the further question, whether blood that has been lost..., or the flesh or hairs that previously existed, shall rise again, or only those we had at the time of death, being pressed in argument they take refuge in saying that we must alow God to do as he wills. The better sort of them, to avoid being driven by their theory to reassemble the very blood which has happened on various occasions to be lost from our bodies, say it is our body in its last state that will rise again.

At this point in the discussion Origen puts the 'chain of consumption' argument to them, and continues:

Whose body then shall it be in the resurrection? And so the result is that we shall go headlong into the depths of nonsense and have not a word to say. After such straits, they take refuge in all things being possible to God. And they bring forward passages of the Scriptures which can by superficial interpretation give support to their views. Such is the passage in Ezekiel, 'And the hand of the Lord was upon me....' [37:1-6] and others [Mt 8:12; Rom 8:11].... Every lover of truth should give independent consideration to these passages and endeavour in regard to the resurrection both to maintain the tradition of the ancients and to avoid falling into the absurdity of beggarly ideas, which are both impossible and unworthy of God.[46]

Origen is not unaware, in spite of his impatience, that his pauline understanding of the spiritual character of the resurrection body seemed to many, particularly to many of

[46] *Psalms, fragment.*

the less well-educated, to be threatening the identity of the raised body and the earthly and so to be destroying "the tradition of the ancients." In this same commentary on the psalm he tries to reassure them—by a candid exposition of his thought—that their personal identity will remain, that the only change will be for the better.

> One principle in this subject must be recognized: that every body which is held together by a nature which assimilates to it certain elements from without by way of nourishment, and gets rid of others in place of what is taken...never retains its material substance the same. Hence it is not a bad name for the body to call it a river. Possibly...the existing substance does not remain the same in our body for even two days. And yet Paul, let us say, or Peter, is always the same, and this not only in his soul, the substance of which is not with us in a state of flux nor ever has fresh elements introduced; he is the same, however fluid may be the nature of the body, because the form [*eidos*] which distinguishes the body is the same....
>
> And further though the bodily form, which at the resurrection is again thrown around the soul, has some resemblance to the form by which Peter or Paul is recognized, yet it changes for the better and it is certainly not this original substance that is still imposed upon it.... So we must conceive for our present subject that the body that is to be will have the same form, though there will be the greatest possible change for the better.[47]

The change for the better—from material to spiritual—will be necessary to inhabit the realm of the spiritual God. Again, Origen argues carefully, this time on the basis of the suitability of a body for its environment.

> For the soul, while it exists in bodily regions, must make use of bodies corresponding to those regions. Just as, if

[47]*Psalms, fragment.*

we had become aquatic creatures and obliged to live in the sea, we should inevitably have had all the other constitution of fishes; so, as we must one day inherit the Kingdom of Heaven and dwell in the regions of bliss, we shall necessarily make use of spiritual bodies, yet the form of the earlier body will not be lost, even though a change to a more glorious condition takes place in it. It was so with the form of Jesus. . .; it did not become in the Transfiguration wholly different from what it was. . . God will one day claim the flesh. But it will be flesh no more, though the features which once existed in the flesh will remain the same features in the spiritual body.[48]

Origen returns once more to the seed sown in the ground to makes his point of the identity of the two bodies in an interesting understanding of the human form imposed on the creation.

The seminal word or reason in the grain of corn lays hold of the surrounding substance, entirely permeates it, takes possession of its form, and implants all its own power in what was once earth, water, air, fire. . . . Thus is the ear of corn perfected, excelling beyond comparison the original grain in size and form and variety.[49]

And, finally, his doctrine of the seminal nature of the identity between the earthly and the heavenly bodies, his conviction of the spiritual nature of the afterlife and of the intellectual contemplation of God which will make that life blessed are all contained in this passage of *Against Celsus*:

The doctrine of the resurrection teaches that the tabernacle of the soul. . .possesses a seminal principle. And in this tabernacle those who are righteous groan, being weighed down, and desiring not to put it off, but to be

---

[48] *Psalms, fragment.*

[49] *Psalms, fragment.*

clothed on top of it.... We do not talk about the resurrection, as Celsus imagines, because we have *misunderstood the doctrine of reincarnation*, but because we know
that when the soul, which in its own nature is incorporeal
and invisible, is in any material place it requires a body
suited to the nature of that environment. In the first
place, it bears this body after it has put off the former
body which was necessary at first but which is not super-
fluous in its second state. In the second place, it puts a
body on top of that which it possessed formerly, because
it needs a better garment for the purer, ethereal, and
heavenly regions.... We shall put on incorruptibility
and immortality which...do not allow the person who
wears them to suffer corruption or death....

We need a body for various purposes because we are in
a material place, and so it needs to be of the same character as that of the nature of the material place, whatever
they may be; and as we require a body, we put the
qualities previously mentioned on top of the tabernacle.
But in order to know God we need no body at all. The
knowledge of God is not derived from the eye of the body,
but from the mind which sees that which is in the image of
the Creator and by divine providence has received the
power to know God. And that which sees God is a pure
heart, from which evil thoughts no longer proceed, nor
murders, nor blasphemies, nor an evil eye, nor any other
evil deed.[50]

Yet in spite of Origen's careful arguments and the
undoubted beauty of his conception of eternal happiness as
the intimate contemplation of God, his teaching on the
resurrection was vigorously attacked.

The Reaction to Origen: Methodius

It has been suggested that the debate which quickly broke

[50]*Celsus* VII.32-33.

out[51] over Origen's views on the resurrection, and which lasted for centuries,[52] was concerned—as were so many of the controversies of the patristic church—with the nature of salvation. Is it essentially an involvement of the human person in the divine life, or an involvement of God in human life?[53] Or is it possible to hold the two in balance? Origen's idea of salvation had been the lifting up of the human person to the realm of the spiritual, because there God dwells, but it seems to have appeared to some that he had abandoned the second, the divinization of earthly life, and, by his emphasis on the spirituality of the resurrection body and the life to come, denied the continuity of that life with human life in this world. Salvation, for Methodius (a bishop of the late third and early fourth century) on the other hand, was the perfecting of earthly life, and it seems that he looked forward to an eternal life which would be that perfected earthly life. In terms of the divinization of this earthly life it is significant that one of his arguments is based on the motive and worth of the Incarnation.

> But if any one were to think that the earthy image is the flesh itself, but the heavenly image some other spiritual body apart from the flesh, let him first consider that Christ, the heavenly man, when he appeared, bore the same form of limbs and the same image of flesh as ours, through which he also, who was not man, became man, that "as in Adam all die, even so in Christ shall all be made alive." For if he bore flesh for any other reason than that of setting the flesh free and raising it up, why did he

[51]Cf. Y.-M. Duval, "Tertullien contre Origene sur la resurrection de la chair," *Revue des Etudes Augustiniennes* 17 (1971) p. 227.

[52]Several tenets of Origen's teaching were condemned at the second Council of Constantinople, 553.

[53]Cf. J. Armantage, "The Best of Both Worlds: Origen's views on Religion and Resurrection," *Origeniana* (Bari: Instituto di Letteratura Cristiana Antico, 1975), 339-347.

> bear flesh superfluously, as he purposed neither to save it,
> nor to raise it up?[54]

Methodius therefore shared Origen's resistance to the
idea of the destruction of the material universe, but for a
different reason. Whereas Origen had looked for a change
of its quality and outward form (cf. above, p. 126, p. 128),
Methodius' hope was for its renewal and perfection.

> [I]t is not satisfactory to say that the universe will be
> utterly destroyed, and sea and air and sky will be no
> longer. For the whole world will be deluged with fire from
> heaven, and burnt for the purpose of purification and
> renewal; it will not however, come to complete ruin and
> corruption. . . . The creation, then, after being restored
> to a better and more seemly state, remains, rejoicing and
> exulting over the children of God at the resurrection. . . .
> For in reality God did not establish the universe in vain,
> or to no purpose but destruction, as those weak-minded
> men say, but to exist and be inhabited and continue.[55]

And again:

> For as the earth is to exist after the present age, there
> must certainly be inhabitants for it who shall no longer be
> liable to death, nor shall marry, nor beget children, but
> live in all happiness, like the angels, without change or
> decay.[56]

The purified earth will be the habitation of the purified
human person, including the body in its fleshly form.
Methodius sees death as the means by which sin will be
destroyed and that perfection achieved.

---

[54] *De Resurrectione* 13. All quotations from *On the Resurrection* are taken from
W.R. Clark, *The Writings of Methodius, Alexander of Lycopolis, Peter of Alex-
andra* (Edinburgh, T. and T. Clark, 1849), slightly altered.

[55] *Res.* 8.

[56] *Res.* 5.

God, the builder, by the timely application of death, checked man, his own temple, when he had sinned,.. in order that the flesh, when sin is withered and dead, may, like a restored temple, be raised up again with the same parts, uninjured and immortal, while sin is utterly and entirely destroyed.[57]

Using the metaphor of a craftsman, Methodius argues that if one were to see a beautiful statue ruined by an envious rival, he could "restore it to its former condition" only by melting it down and recasting it.

[I]f he should wish it to be perfectly beautiful and fault-less, it must be broken up and recast, in order that all the scars and mutilations inflicted upon it by treachery and envy, may be got rid of by the breaking up and recasting of it, while the image is restored again uninjured and unalloyed to the same form as before, and made as like itself as possible. For it is impossible for an image under the hands of the original artist to be lost. . . . Now God's plan seems to me to have been the same as that which prevails among ourselves. For seeing man, his fairest work, corrupted by envious treachery, he could not endure, with his love for man, to leave him in such a condition, lest he should be for ever faulty, and bear the blame to eternity; but he dissolved him again into his original materials in order that, by remodelling, all the blemishes in him might waste away and disappear.[58]

It will be 'the original artist' who will restore the human body; Methodius is thus using the traditional argument that a second creation would be no more outside the power of God than the first.[59]

---

[57] *Res.* 6.

[58] *Res..* 9.

[59] *Res.* 14.

Methodius, it is clear, had no patience with Origen's argument that the resurrection body will be a spiritual one, nor the reason Origen was said to have given for that view: that the body is a fetter on the soul. Methodius insists on the permanence, but not the permanent corruptibility, of the human body.

> But it is evidently absurd to think that the body will not co-exist with the soul in the eternal state, because it is a bond of fetters. [Some argue this] so that... we who are to live in the kingdom of light may not be forever condemned to be slaves of corruption.[60]

His point is that a spiritual resurrection body is not the only way to ensure freedom from corruption. Methodius' exegesis of 1 Cor 15:50 ("flesh and blood cannot possess the kingdom of God") is that the kingdom of God, which is eternal life, is not possessed by the body, but rather the body is possessed by eternal life. Thus the body may be in the possession of incorruption, but it may not possess incorruption.[61]

> [Therefore as] the statement [has been] refuted in which [Origen and his followers] defined the flesh to be the soul's chain, the argument also is destroyed, that the flesh will not rise again, lest, if we resume it, we will be prisoners in the kingdom of light.[62]

In another argument against the completely spiritual nature of the resurrection life, Methodius appeals that to the order of the universe, that is that God created several orders of immortal beings, and one order does not depart from its form to assume that of another.

> For Christ at his coming did not proclaim that the human nature should, when it is immortal, be remoulded or

[60]*Res.* 3.
[61]*Res.* 13.
[62]*Res.* 3.

transformed into another nature, but into what it was before the fall. For each one among created things must remain in its own proper place, that none may be wanting to any....[63]

Methodius argues that to deny the resurrection of the corporeal body is to deny the resurrection altogether, and this conviction on his part seems to have been at the heart of his resistance to Origen's teaching on the resurrection.

> For it is not that which is not dead, but that which is dead, which is laid down. But it is the flesh which dies; the soul is immortal. So, then, if the soul be immortal, and the body be that which is dead, those who say that there is a resurrection, but not of the flesh, deny any resurrection; because it is not that which remains standing, but that which has fallen and been laid down, which is set up....[64]

The "setting up" is the restoration of life to the corporeal body, but this time with the gifts of incorruptibility and immortality. Methodius' point is that flesh is in itself neither corruptible nor incorruptible, but takes on one or other characteristic in different circumstances—corruption through sin, incorruption through God's salvific power.

> [F]lesh was made to border on incorruption and corruption, being itself neither the one nor the other, and, though it was the work and property of incorruption, it was overcome by corruption for the sake of [its own] pleasure. Therefore it became corruptible, and was laid in the dust of the earth. When, then, it was overcome by corruption, and delivered over to death through disobedience, God did not leave it to corruption, to be tri-

---

[63]*Res.* 10.
[64]*Res.* 12.

umphed over as a possession, but, after conquering death
by the resurrection, delivered it again to incorruption.[65]

Methodius' concern may indeed have been the character
of salvation, as was suggested earlier, but it may equally
have been the personal survival of the individual human
person. The two are not incompatible and, if 'real' is understood as convertible with 'material,' one demands the other.
It has pointed out the Methodius badly misunderstood
Origen's notion of *eidos*. Whereas Origen meant it to
express precisely the identity of the spiritual body with the
earthly (although with qualitative differences), Methodius
did not appreciate the philosophical underpinnings of Origen's notion and thought that he was teaching that the risen
body would be other than the earthly, that is, that there
would be no continuity of what would today would be called
'personality.'[66]

[65]*Res.* 13.

[66]H. Grouzel, "Les critiques adressees par Method e et ses contemporains a la
doctrine origenienne du corps ressuscite," *Gregorianum* 53 (1972), 679-716.

6. THE FOURTH CENTURY

The fourth century church had other issues to deal with (as it gained imperial recognition) and other theological topics to debate, (of a trinitarian and christological nature) and the controversy about the resurrection of the body occupied less of the attention of the writers of that period. Speculation about the nature of the risen body and life eternal did not disappear entirely, however, as will be seen in the case of Gregory of Nyssa, and the quarrel flared up again at the end of the century in the exchanges among Jerome, Rufinus and John, bishop of Jerusalem. We have also writings from the fourth century which shed a more positive light on the resurrection hope of Christians—catechetical instructions (from, for example, Theodore of Mopsuestia) and letters of consolation (from, for example, Basil and Gregory of Nazianzus).

The revival of the quarrel about the resurrection body at the end of the century was not conducted on a very serious theological level, and is worth attention only because it reveals the widespread perception that orthodoxy required the affirmation of the resurrection of the 'flesh,' rather than the body. The quarrel was touched off again by the zeal of bishop Epiphanius, and it has been suggested that the motive (apart from his general concern for orthodoxy) was his fear that the extreme asceticism of egyptian monasticism was one "which sought freedom from man's corporeal tradition."[1] Ephiphanius saw the origenist theory of the resurrection body as an expression of this disdain of the body and adopted Methodius' harsh attack uncritically. Ephiphanius was not himself a theologican of stature, but, by laying the charge of heresy against Origen (whom he also associated with arianism), and especially by preaching publicly against his doctrine in Jerusalem in 393, he drew others into the battle. The conflict was as much one of personalities as of issues; the alacrity with which Jerome repudiated Origen, whom he had earlier admired, is one of history's mild puzzles. In any case, the situation elicited statements on the resurrection, and particularly on the resurrection body, from several prominent churchmen and brought the issue once again to the public eye.

In 397, in a letter to Pammachius, Jerome accused Origen of deception: "though he nine times speaks of the resurrection of the body, he has not once introduced the resurrection of the flesh, and you may fairly suspect that he left it out on purpose."[2] This distinction between 'body' and 'flesh' was at the heart of Epiphanius' concern: could any resurrection be real which was not material, that is, fleshly? The letter ended with an earnest call for John, bishop of Jerusalem, to repent of the origenist heresy he held. (John had previously defended himself against a similar charge from Epiphanius, in a sermon preached in 395, in which he affirmed the reality of the resurrection body.) In 399 Jerome wrote a public letter, with Rufinus (who had accused Jerome of Origenism) as its target. In it Jerome disavowed any admiration for Origen as a theologian, and asserted his own orthodoxy in trinitarian doctrines. His concern was, however, what he perceived to be a deliberate ambiguity.

---

[1] J.F. Dechow. *Dogma and Mysticism in Early Christianity: Ephiphanius of Cyprus and the Legacy of Origen* (Ann Arbor: Xerox University Microfilms, 1975), 317.

[2] *Letter to Pammachius against John of Jerusalem*, 25. Quotations from Jerome's letters are taken from W.H. Freemantle *Letters of Jerome* (Grand Rapids: Eerdmans, 1982).

There are some who believe, they say, in the resurrection of the body. This confession, if only it be sincere, is free from objection. But as there are bodies celestial and bodies terrestial...they use the word 'body' instead of the word 'flesh' in order that an orthodox person hearing them say 'body' may take them to mean 'flesh,' while a heretic will understand that they mean 'spirit.'

And when we inquire whether the resurrection will exhibit anew the hair and the teeth, the chest and the stomach, the hands and the feet, and all the other members of the body, then, no longer able to contain their mirth, they burst out laughing and tell us that in that case we shall need barbers, and cakes, and doctors and cobblers. Do you, they ask us in turn, believe that after the resurrection men's cheeks will still be rough and those of women smooth, and that sex will differentiate their bodies as at present? Then if we admit this, they at once deduce from our admission conclusions involving the grossest materialism.[3]

Jerome accused those who denied the resurrection of the flesh as hating it. "I do not despise," he wrote, "the flesh in which Christ was born and rose again, or scorn the mud which, now baked into a clean vessel, reigns in heaven."[4]

Rufinus' defence directed to Anastasius, bishop of Rome, began, a circumstances of the time required, with a defence of the correctness of his trinitarian views. In it he continues:

I confess...that [the Son of God] has taken upon him our natural human flesh and soul; that in this he suffered and was buried and rose again from the dead; that the flesh in which he rose was that same flesh which had been laid in the sepulchre; and that in this same flesh, together with the soul, he ascended into heaven after his resurrec-

[3]*Ep.* 84.5.
[4]*Ep.* 84.8.

tion: from whence we look for his coming to judge the quick and the dead.

But, further, as to the resurrection of our own flesh, I believe that it will be in its integrity and perfection; it will be this very flesh in which we now live. We do not hold, as is slanderously reported by some men, that another flesh will rise instead of this; but this very flesh, without the loss of a single member, . . . none whatever of all its properties will be absent except its corruptibility.[5]

In a later defence, in 401, Rufinus compares the resurrection body of Christians to that of Christ.

It must be evident that whatever the members—hair, flesh, bones—were in which Christ rose, in the same shall we also rise. For this purpose he offered himself to the disciples to touch after his resurrection, so that no hesitation as to his resurrection should remain. . . . Who can be so mad as to think that he himself will rise otherwise than as he rose who opened the door of the resurrection?[6]

Jerome had ridiculed some women who wished to rise not "in their poor weak bodies," and Rufinus replied, "Are not these poor women after all more right than you when they say that their bodily fraility cannot have dominion over them in the world beyond?" He continues:

[The Jews] believe that they will rise, but in such sort as that they will enjoy all carnal delights and luxuries and other pleasures of the body. What else, indeed, can this 'bodily frailty' of yours mean except members given over to corruption, appetites stimulated and lusts inflamed.[7]

[5]*Rufinus' Apology* (addressed to Anastasius, bishop of Rome), 3-4. Quotation of Rufinus are taken from W.H. Freemantle, *The Writings of Rufinus* (Grand Rapids: Eerdmans, 1982).

[6]*Apology of Rufinus* (addressed to Apronianus), 6.

[7]*Apol.* (Apronianus), 7,8.

Accusations such as that may have lain behind Jerome's phrase, 'grossest materialism.'

Other writings in the fourth century were of more positive value to the theology of the resurrection. A good deal of Gregory of Nyssa's writing was devoted to the eternal destiny of the Christian, and he is considered to have made a significant contribution to the debate concerning the resurrection of the body.[8] The interesting suggestion has been made that Gregory in his earlier years had difficulty with the idea of the resurrection of the body, and that this difficulty is reflected in his treatise, *On the Dead*.[9] There he argues that the soul is what constitutes the human person, that the body is in conflict with it, and that, consequently, death is a release for the soul. In that treatise however, his "most original and adventurous contribution,"[10] is put forward by the adaptation to a Christian context of oriental thinking on reincarnation—that the form of the resurrection body will be determined by personal characteristics, good and bad.

> Perhaps someone will not be wholly wrong if he says that the distinctive form of each individual will be provided by the nature of his moral character, whatever that may be. At present the interaction of the elements determine the different characteristics of individuals, with each gaining his shape or the colour of his complexion according to the balance of the corresponding elements. But, it seems to me, the factors determining the form of each person then will not be these elements. Instead his qualities of evil or virtue will become explicit, and their particular combination will create the form.[11]

---

[8] I am indebted in this section to an excellent study by T.J. Dennis, "Gregory on the Resurrection of the Body," in A. Spira and C. Klock, eds. *The Easter Sermons of Gregory of Nyssa: Translation and Commentary* (Cambridge, Mass.: Philadelphia Patristic Foundation, 1981), 55-80.

[9] Dennis, 69-71.

[10] Dennis, 64.

[11] *De Mortuis*, translation Dennis, 66-67.

Whatever his earlier position, in *On the Creation of Man*, written in 379 or 380, Gregory presents several arguments for the possibility of the resurrection. His first is that good triumphs over evil and

> [That] paradise therefore will be restored, that tree will be restored which is in truth the tree of life, and there will be restored the grace of the image and the dignity of rule. It does not seem to me that our hope is for those things which are now subjected by God to man for the necessary uses of life, but for another kingdom, of a description that belongs to mysteries beyond speech.[12]

Gregory explains that the resurrection cannot take place until "the...complement of human nature" has been filled,[13] and that Christ's miracles of raising the dead described in scripture are the strongest possible argument for God's power. In contrast to his speaking of the spiritual nature of the life to come in the passage just quoted, his words here come close to suggesting revivification of the material body, although the general trend of his thought was completely different.

> Since, then, every prediction of the Lord is shown to be true by the testimony of events, and we have not only learned this by his words, but also received the proof of the promise in his deeds—from those very persons who returned to life by resurrection—, what grounds are left to those who disbelieve?[14]

Gregory advances the usual arguments for the possibility of the resurrection—the seed in the ground and the initiation of human life—concluding "that the preaching of the resur-

---

[12] *De hominis opificio* 21.4. All quotations from this treatise are taken from W. Moore and H.A. Moore, *Select Writings and Letters of Gregory, Bishop of Nyssa* (New York: The Christian Literature Company, 1983), slightly altered.

[13] *De hom. opif.* 22.6.

[14] *De hom. opif.* 25.13.

rection contains nothing beyond those facts which are known to us experimentally."[15]

It was in this treatise that Gregory adapted Origen's notion of the *eidos* in an interesting way. Dennis points out that "for Origen *eidos* is the one distinct element of the earthly body to be preserved in the resurrection...For Gregory...the *eidos* is what provides the means for reassembly of the body's atoms."[16] Gregory sees the *eidos* as the characteristic mark the soul imprints on the materials of the body (he makes the comparison with cattle which can be separated out from the herd by their owner).

> [A]s the soul is disposed to cling to and long for the body that has been wedded to it, there also attaches to it in a hidden way a certain close relationship and power of recognition as a result of their mingling, as though some marks had been imprinted by nature.[17]

He compares the marks to a seal.

> The form remains in the soul as in the impression of a seal, and those elements which have received from the seal [its] impression...will not fail to be recognized by the soul.[18]

At the resurrection the soul will receive all those elements which correspond to the stamp of its form, Gregory explains.

While *The Creation of Man* had as its aim meeting the arguments of those who denied the possibility of the resurrection, in *On the Soul and the Resurrection* Gregory presents his understanding of the life of the Christian after death. The occasion was the death of Basil, and the genre a

---

[15]*De hom. opif.* 27.8.
[16]Dennis, 59.
[17]*De hom. opif.* 27.2.
[18]*De hom. opif.* 27.5.

dialogue between Gregory and his sister, Macrina (who has been seen as the voice of the church's teaching).[19] The treatise begins by acknowledging the human fear of death and the difficulties (expressed by Gregory) of proving the immortality of the soul: "How can we arrive at some steadfast and unchanging opinion concerning the soul's immortality?"[20] In her reply Macrina explains the relation of the soul to the body and, in doing so, touches on the question of the resurrection of the body:

> [My] opinion about [the soul] is. . . that it is a substance which is begotten, alive, intelligible, and, by itself, it puts into an organic perceptive body a life-giving power as long as the nature capable of receiving these things endures.[21]

> In the case of living bodies in which there is substance resulting from the mingling of the elements, there is, according to the logic of being, nothing in common between the simple and invisible essence of the soul and the coarseness of the body. Nevertheless, it is not doubted that the vital energy of the soul is present in the elements, diffused with a logic that is beyond human comprehension. Therefore, when the elements in the body are resolved into themselves, that which links it together through its vital energy does not perish.[22]

> The soul knows the individual elements which formed the body in which it dwelt, even after the dissolution of those elements. Even if nature drags them far apart from each other and, because of their basic differences prevents

[19]*On the Soul and the Resurrection*. Translated by V.W. Callahan, *Saint Gregory of Nyssa: Ascetical Works* (Washington: Catholic University of America, 1967), 198-272. All quotations of *On the Soul and the Resurrection* are taken from this translation.

[20]*De Anima*, 200.

[21]*De Anima*, 205.

[22]*De Anima*, 213.

each of them from mixing with its opposite, the soul will, nevertheless, exist along with each element, fastening upon what is its own by its power of knowing it and it will remain there until the union of the separated parts occurs again in the reforming of the dissolved being which is properly called 'the resurrection.'[23]

Accepting Macrina's argument, Gregory says:

"You seem to me...to give excellent support to the doctrine of the resurrection. It should be possible through these arguments to persuade those who are reluctant to accept it because they do not think it possible for the elements to come back together again and produce the same man.[24]

Macrina develops her point more fully, taking into account the fear of the loss of personal identity, and using the analogy of pieces of shattered jars which can be identified by their owners.

One hears people...asking how, since the dissolution of the elements according to their kinds is complete, the element of heat [the soul] in a person, once it has mingled generally with its own kind, can be withdrawn again for the purpose of reforming a man. For, they would say, unless the very same element returns the result would be a similar being and not the individual himself, that is to say, another person would come into being and such a process would not be a resurrection, but the creation of a new man. But, if the original is to be reconstituted, it is necessary for it to be entirely the same, taking up its original nature in all the parts of its elements.

Therefore, as I said, such an opinion about the soul

[23] *De Anima*, 229.

[24] *De Anima*, 230; cf. Dennis, 56 concerning the methodian legacy of the necessity of identity of substance, form and structure of the risen body with the earthly one.

would be a sufficient rebuttal to this objection. Even after the dissolution of the elements in which it existed from the beginning, the soul, like a guardian of what is its own, remains in them and, even when it is mingled with the general mass, it does not give up its individuality in the subtlety and mobility of its intellectual power.... [T]hrough the unique force of the soul, when the different elements are drawn together and when what was once the core of our body is reconstituted by the soul, each part is folded again into its former accustomed place and embraces what is familiar to it.[25]

Gregory wishes to pursue the question of the resurrection of the body:

It is clear that somehow, as a consequence of what we have been saying, the dogma of the resurrection has come into our discussion, a dogma which seems to me to be true and worthy of belief from the teaching of Scripture and not to be doubted. However, since the weakness of human thought relies somehow on more accessible arguments for such belief, I think we should not leave this point without consideration.[26]

Macrina outlines non-Christian beliefs of the afterlife and raises the question of the origin of the soul: "Scripture has dismissed our meddlesome query about the 'how' because it is impossible to know. So it is left to us to investigate the question...."[27] Towards the end of the treatise she presents her understanding of the nature of resurrection life, beginning with an allegorical reading of some of the passages, from the hebrew scriptures, e.g. Psalm 117.27:

"a general feast will be established around God by those

[25] *De Anima*, 230.
[26] *De Anima*, 245.
[27] *De Anima*, 254.

who have been clothed through the resurrection and there will be one and the same joy for all. No longer will there be different degrees of participation in the reasoning nature.[28]

But, Gregory demurs, there are hard questions to be asked:

[I]f our human bodies return to life in the same condition in which they left it, then man is looking forward to endless misfortune in the resurrection [old age, disease, infanticide].[29]

[But] unless the body is brought back to life as it was when it was mingled with the earth, the dead person will not have risen, but the earth will have been formed again into another man.[30]

Giving an example of remembering an old man (the description is graphic, Basil, perhaps?) and of meeting the same person as a young man in the afterlife, Gregory picks up the theme of the fluidity of human life (Origen's river).

As long as life continues, there is no stop, for it is either increasing or decreasing or forever going from one state to another. If someone is not the same as he was yesterday, but becomes someone else through the process of change, when the resurrection brings our body to life, a kind of all-inclusive man will come into being so that nothing of the resurrected person will be missing in the risen person, the newly-born, the infant, the child, the adolescent, the man, the father, the old man, and all the stages in between.[31]

---

[28] *De Anima*, 259.
[29] *De Anima*, 261.
[30] *De Anima*, 262.
[31] *De Anima*, 263.

Macrina handles this difficulty by explaining that eternal life will have shed all connotations of the temporal and the sinful.

> [T]he resurrection is the restoring of our nature to its former condition. At the beginning of life...there was neither old age...nor infancy nor sickness...nor any of the other bodily miseries. For it is not likely that God would create such things. Human nature was something divine before humanity inclined itself to evil.... [O]ur nature. once it is involved in the disease of sin, necessarily suffers the consequences of sin. But when it returns to undiseased blessedness, it will no longer be affected by the consequences of evil.[32]

She continues:

> Just as one who is wearing a torn garment takes it off and no longer connects the ugliness of what he has discarded with himself, so we shall be when we have put off that dead and ugly garment made of the skins of irrationality. I here equate the word 'skin' with the aspects of the animal nature with which we clothe ourselves when we become accustomed to sin [sexual intercourse, conception, childbearing, sordidness, the nursing and nurturing of children, elimination, the process of growing up, the prime of life, growing old, disease, and death]. If that skin no longer envelops us, how can those things connected with it continue to exist in us?[33]

The seed metaphor again proves useful:

> For as the seed, after it is dissolved in the soil and leaves behind its quantitative deficiency and qualitative peculiarity of form, does not give up being itself, but remains itself although it becomes a stalk of grain which differs

[32]*De Anima*, 256-6.
[33]*De Anima* 266.

very much from itself in size and beauty and variety and form; in the same way, human nature also lets go in death all the peculiar characteristics it acquired through its sinful disposition. I mean dishonor, corruption, weakness, differing ages, but it does not give up being itself although it changes over into a spiritual and sinless condition.... None of the beauties we see not...will be destroyed in the life to come.[34]

The joy of the life to come is, in Macrina's understanding, the contemplation of divine beauty, but that will be possible only for the purified soul:

For [God] the one goal is this, the perfection of the universe through each man individually, the fulfillment of our nature. Some of us are purged of evil in this life, some are cured of it through fire in the afterlife, some have not had the experience of good and evil in life here. God proposes for everyone a participation in the goods in himself which scripture says: "eye has not seen, nor ear heard, nor has it entered into the mind of man." In my opinion, this is nothing other than existing in God himself....[35]

Evil is not only sin, but the concerns of this life, and they too must be shed. Macrina speaks of them as bonds:

When the chains (so to speak) around the soul are broken, its ascent to the good is light and free, since no bodily weight is dragging it down. But if anyone is entirely preoccupied with the things of the flesh and uses every movement of the soul and all its energy for his fleshly desires, he will not be separated from experiences involving the flesh, even when he is out of it.[36]

[34] *De Anima*, 269-70.
[35] *De Anima*, 267.
[36] *De Anima*, 236.

Gregory points out an apparent contradiction:

> Since every irrational impulse in us is removed after
> purgation, the desiring faculty will no longer exist, but, if
> this is so, there will be no inclination towards what is
> better, since the soul will no longer have a desire for the
> good.[37]

But Macrina is ready with her answer:

> [The reply is] that the faculty of contemplation and of
> making distinctions is characteristic of the god-like por-
> tion of the soul, since, by these, we comprehend even the
> divine. When, either because of our effort here on earth
> or because of our purgation afterwards, our soul is freed
> from its associations with the emotions, we shall in no
> way be impeded in our contemplation of the beautiful.
> The beautiful, by its very nature, is somehow attractive to
> everyone looking at it. If the soul is freed from all evil, it
> will exist entirely in the realm of the beautiful. But beauti-
> ful is the divine to which the soul will be joined on
> account of its purity, uniting with what is proper to it. If
> this occurs, there will no longer be a need for any move-
> ment based on desire to lead us to the beautiful.[38]

A question that will become acute in Augustine—the reason
for the presence of the risen body in heaven—is implicit in
this treatise. Macrina speaks in so disparaging a manner of
the earthly body that the reader wonders if anything other
than obedience to the Church's teaching impels her to find a
place for it—no matter how changed—in the after life. To
put it plainly, what use and function will the body serve
there?

It is worth recalling that the treatise, *On the Soul and the
Resurrection*, was occasioned by the death of Basil, and that

[37] *De Anima*, 237.
[38] *De Anima*, 237.

Macrina's arguments and assertions were designed to comfort and reassure Gregory. We have several examples from the fourth century (although none so fully developed as Nyssa's treatise) of letters of consolation written to bereaved Christians, and "[t]he assertion that Christians, unlike the rest of mankind, [had] a solid basis for hope in the face of death was both the starting point...and the concluding argument for these consolers."[39] The first example of such a letter included here is from Basil to his friend, Nectarius, on the death of his son. He begins by appealing to the realistic and reasonable expectations of human life which should beheld.

> If, however, we wish to make use of God's gift, which He has implanted within our hearts, we shall be comforted. By his gift I mean that sober reason, which knows how, both in fair weather to keep our souls within bounds, and, when the sky is more cloudy, to remind us of the lot of man, suggesting to us (what we have already both seen and heard) that life is full of such afflictions, that the examples of human misfortune are many.[40]

The second appeal is to trust in Christ and the promise of the resurrection, a trust which is based on a trust in God's providence generally:

> [A]bove all, that it is God's command that those who put their trust in Christ shall not grieve for those who have been laid to rest, because of their hope of the resurrection, and again, that for great endurance great crowns of glory await us at the hands of the Judge. If, then, we permit reason to whisper to us these reminders, perchance we

---

[39]Cf. R. Gregg, *Consolation Philosophy: Greek and Christian Paideia in Basil and the Two Gregories* (Cambridge, Mass.: Philadelphia Patristic Foundation, 1975), 156.

[40]*Ep.* V. All quotations from Basil's letters are taken from R.J. Deferrari, *Saint Basil, 'The Letters'* (Cambridge, Mass.: Harvard University Press, 1972).

shall find some slight relief from our trouble. Wherefore I exort you, as a noble contestant, to stand firm against the blow, however great, and not to fall under the weight of your grief, nor yet to lose your courage, having assurance that even if the reasons for God's ordinances elude us, yet surely that which is ordained by Him who is wise and who loves us must be accepted, even if it be painful. For He Himself knows how He dispenses to each that which is best for him, and for what reason He sets for us unequal terms of life. For there exists a reason, incomprehensible to man, why some are sooner taken hence, while others are left behind to persevere for a longer time in this life of sorrows.[41]

And the final comfort is that the child has reached the haven towards which all Christians are hastening, that he is now in the state of purity which is the goal of the life of virtue:

We have not been bereft of the boy, but we have given him back to the lender; nor has his life been destroyed, but merely transformed for the better; earth has not covered our beloved one, but heaven has received him. Let us abide a brief space, and we shall be with him whose loss we mourn. Nor will the period of separation be great, since in this life, as on a journey, we are all hastening to the same abode; and although one has already taken up his lodging there, and another has just arrived, and another is hastening thither, yet the same goal will receive us all. For even though your son has finished his journey first, nevertheless we shall all travel the same path, and the same hospice awaits us all. Only may God grant that we through virtue may become like to him in purity, that by the blamelessness of our character we may obtain the same repose as the children of Christ.[42]

[41] *Ep.* V.
[42] *Ep.* V.

Another letter, written perhaps to console a recent widow, sounds the same note of death as a happy release from the temptations of earthly life, and recalls that "the hope of Christians" lies elsewhere; in it the resurrection, however, is not explicitly mentioned:

> For even if we are ignorant of the words according to which everything that happens is brought to us as a blessing from God, yet we should at least be convinced of this—that assuredly whatever happens is good, either for us through the reward won by our patience or for the soul which we have received, lest by tarrying longer in this world the soul be contaminated by the wickedness which inheres in human life. For if the hope of Christians were limited to this life, the early separation from the body would reasonably be thought hard; but if for those who live according to God the beginning of the true life is the release of the soul from these bodily bounds, why then are we sorrowful even as those who have no hope? Therefore, I beg you, do not succumb to your woes, but show that you stand above them and have transcended them.[43]

Gregory of Nazianzus, *Oration* 7, written on the death of his brother, Caesar, is a much more moving letter of consolation than those of Basil. Here Gregory sounds the themes we have come to expect: Caesar will not have the joys and satisfactions of those who live a longer life (wealth, children, learning), but he will escape the dark side of those gifts as well (abuse of power, bereavement, mental disquiet). Gregory continues:

> Is this inadequate for our consolation? I will add a more potent remedy. I believe the words of the wise that every fair soul loved by God, set free from the bonds of the body, when it leaves this world and departs hence, at once enjoys a sense and perception of the blessings which await it, inasmuch as that which darkened it has been purged

[43] *Ep.* CI.

away or laid aside . . . and it feels a wondrous pleasure and exultation. . . . Then, a little later, it receives its kindred flesh, which once shared in its pursuits of things above, from the earth which both gave and had been entrusted with it. In some way known to God, who knit [the soul and body] together and dissolved them, [the body] enters with [the soul] upon the inheritance of the glory there. And, as shared, through their close union, in [the body's] hardships, so also it bestows upon it a portion of its joys, gathering up entirely into itself, and becoming with it one in spirit and in mind and in God, the mortal and mutable being swallowed up by life. . . .

Why am I faint-hearted in my hopes? Why do I behave like a mere creature of a day? I await the voice of the Archangel, the last trumpet, the transformation of the heavens, the transfiguration of the earth, the liberation of the elements, the renovation of the universe. Then I shall see Caesarius himself, no longer in exile, no longer laid upon a bier, no longer the object of mourning and pity, but brilliant, glorious, heavenly, such as in my dreams I have often beheld you, dearest and most loving of brothers, pictured thus by my desire, if not by the very truth.[44]

Another source of our information about the fourth century Church's understanding of resurrection, outside the context of controversy, are the instructions given by bishops to their catechumens, later written down and published. Because of the circumstances—the preparation for baptism—it was appropriate that the tie between baptism and resurrection be brought to the catechumens' attention. The following is from Theodore of Mopsuestia.

It is in that faith [that Christ has done away with death] that we approach him and are baptized, because we wish to share from now on in his death, in the hope of sharing

[44]*Oratio* VII.21. This quotation is taken from C.G. Browne and J.E. Swallow, *Select Writings of Gregory of Nazianzus* (New York: the Christian Literature Company, 1894), 236, slightly altered.

in those same good things, namely to rise from the dead in the same manner that he has risen. For that reason, when I am baptized, by immersing my head, it is the death of our Lord Christ which I receive, and his burial which I wish to take upon myself; and there, truly, I already confess the resurrection of our Lord whilst in raising my head as a kind of figure, I perceive myself to be already raised.[45]

The effects of the resurrection of Christ are described:

The resurrection put the seal on all the wonders worked in the economy of Christ, and [it was] the most capital blow among all the righting of wrongs which he effected. By means of [the resurrection] death was destroyed, corruption dissolved, the passions [made to] disappear, mutability done away with, the urgings of sin extinguished, the power of Satan and the violence of demons was destroyed and the anguish of the law was overcome. To all this [is added] the promise of life eternal and immutable.[46]

Quoting 1 Corinthians 15:13-14, Theodore compares Christ's resurrection to that of the Christian:

If it is not indeed possible that the dead are raised, it is clear that neither was Christ raised, for he also, in his body, was the same [human] nature, and it was according to the law of nature that he suffered death. But if we confess that Christ was raised, it is evidently certain that there is in truth a resurrection, because that which cannot happen could not have happened in him. But if it was realized in him, it is clear and certain that it can happen.[47]

[45]*Cat. Hom.* XIV.5. Quotations from Theodore's catechetical homilies are translated from *Les Homelies Catechetiques de Theodore de Mopsueste.* Translated into french [from syriac] by R. Tonneau and R. Devreese (Vatican City: Biblioteca Apostolica Vaticana, 1961).

[46]*Cat. Hom.* VII.4.

[47]*Cat. Hom.* VII.5.

Ever the biblical theologian, Theodore notes that all the evangelists had told of the resurrection, but that only Luke had continued and presented Christ's ascension to heaven.

> For, since it was not only by his resurrection that Christ was for us the first fruits, but also by his ascension to heaven, and that he associated us with him in both by his grace, it is appropriate that we learn about both.[48]

Paul also taught (Philippians 3:20-21) that the bodies of Christians will share the glory of that of Christ:

> It is to heaven that we will be led, from where Christ our Lord will come, who will transform us by the resurrection from the dead, effecting in us a likeness to his body and causing us to mount to heaven to be forever with him.[49]

Life with Christ will follow only upon his judgement:

> [The creed says] 'and he will come again to judge the living and the dead' to teach us of [Christ's] second coming, when once more, we shall be associated with him.... At the moment when he comes, he will raise us all; those who have lived since Adam, all those who have passed on, he will transform to immortal nature.... [N]o one will escape judgement and, once judged [will] receive the retribution which their actions deserve—some blessings, others evils. All will be selected and judged according to that which their will would have chosen.[50]

'Immortality' and 'immutability' were key words for Theodore's eschatological hope, and they are prominent in his description of that eternal life with Christ which will be the reward of the just.

[48]*Cat. Hom.* VII.7.
[49]*Cat. Hom.* VII.8.
[50]*Cat. Hom.* VII.11.

Now that which [Paul] calls 'Jerusalem on high' [Galatians 4:27] is the heavenly dwelling where, by resurrection from the dead, we will be born and will become immortal and immutable, truly revelling in liberty in true joy, violence will no longer afflict us, nor sadness touch us any longer; but [there] we will live in indescribable blessedness and delights which will never end.[51]

7. AUGUSTINE ON THE RESURRECTION

Augustine was clear, adamant and frequently vehement in his assertion that the bodily death of the human person is the result of Adam's sin. No other writer of the age made so important a theological point of it as he did. He wrote, for example, in *Against Fortunatus*:

> The law of death is that by which it was said to the first man, 'You are dust and unto dust you shall return,' for we are all born of him in that state because we are dust and we shall return to dust as a punishment for the sin of the first man.[1]

Not only did Adam's sin bring about human bodily mortality; but, as Augustine worked out his theories of sin and grace, he came to trace the death of the soul, which is the condition of all human persons without the grace of Christ (that is, the state of generic sin), to that primal sin.[2] To parallel this twofold death Augustine taught a twofold

---

[1] *Against Fortunatus* 22.

[2] Cf. W. Babcock, "Augustine's interpretation of Romans A.D. 394-396," *Aug. St.* 10 (1979), 55-74, and J. P. Burns, *The Development of Augustine's Doctrine of Operative Grace* (Paris: Etudes Augustiniennes, 1980).

resurrection, but it is evident that his understanding of the two resurrections—that of the soul and that of the body— did not come with equal ease. The reason for the imbalance is one that has been evident in earlier writers and lies in the theory of what the human person is and in what his or her true happiness lies. In Augustine's thought the soul's conversion, or resurrection (which, like that of the body, was intimately tied to the life, death and resurrection of Christ), is a conversion to right order, away from the lesser goods of this material world and to contemplation of Truth, a contemplation which even in this life (imperfect as it must be) is true wisdom.[3] Augustine's difficulty lay in finding a role for the body in the attainment and, even more, in the enjoyment of this Truth, which could justify its resurrection. The difficulty was not a new one, but Augustine discussed it at greater length than his precedessors. It cannot be said that intellectually he ever completely resolved his difficulties. To the end, the resurrection of the body remained for him largely a matter of faith, minimally buttressed by arguments of reason.

The first mention in Augustine's writings of the resurrection of the body (in *On the Grandeur of the Soul* in 388) is precisely in this context of the soul's contemplation of truth, and with the intimation that he finds this doctrine difficult (as he did that other doctrine which attests the goodness of the human body, the Incarnation). Outlining the stages of the soul's activities from the lowest—the animation and unification of the body—to the highest—contemplation, he notes that a necessary condition for the last is the turning away from the whole material world, including the body.[4] He writes of this last stage when complete detachment is achieved:

> We then shall realize how full of truth are the things we
> are commanded to believe... We shall see that this cor-

---

[3]This theme begins at Cassiciacum and continues throughout all his writings.
[4]*On the Grandeur of the Soul* 33.73.

> poreal nature... undergoes so many changes and altera-
> tions [for the better] that we may hold even the
> resurrection of the body to be so certain as the rising of
> the sun.... [The delights of the contemplation of truth
> will be such] that the death which earlier one feared will
> be desired as the last and best gift, [because] death is the
> flight and escape in every way from this body. [The soul
> after death] will be less impeded from clinging whole-
> heartedly to absolute Truth [than it was even by the
> disciplined body which is the concomitant of the soul that
> reaches contemplation in this life].[5]

Augustine's understanding of the relation of the soul to
the body changed somewhat throughout the 390s,[6] but he
was constant in the conviction expressed in *On the Grandeur of the Soul* that true knowledge was not sense knowledge, or even knowledge derived through the senses.[7] In
such a psychology the soul is independent of, or (as we have
seen) even hampered by, the body in its search for true
wisdom and happiness. A text from *On Music*, probably
dating from ca 395, is illustrative.

> Bodies are better to the extent that they are enriched [by,
> for instance, sensible harmonies], but the soul becomes
> better in depriving [itself] of those things it receives from
> the body when it turns from the bodily senses and reforms
> itself by the divine harmonies of Wisdom.[8]

The context of the passage is the relative excellence of
producing sounds, hearing them, forming harmonies,
remembering sounds and harmonies and judging them.
Judgement clearly comes first, but, in ranking the others,

[5]*Grandeur* 33.76.

[6]For his earlier understanding cf. R.J. O'Connell, *St. Augustine's Early Theory
of Man, A.D. 386-391* (Cambridge, Mass.: Belknap Press, 1968).

[7]Cf. e.g. *The Teacher XIV, 46, The Literal Meaning of Genesis (in twelve books)*
VII.xiv,20, *On the Trinity* VIII.vi.9.

[8]*On Music* VI.iv.7.

Augustine and his pupil engage in a discussion of the possible incongruity of an effect (memory) being more excellent than its cause (the sound itself). Augustine points out that the more truly extraordinary thing is that the body (hearing the sound) has the power to affect the soul (remembering that sound) and he suggests that this disorderly situation is the result of the first sin.

> Wonder, rather, that the body is able to do anything to the soul. Perhaps this would not have been the situation if, after the first sin, the body, which the soul [before Adam's sin] had animated and governed easily and with no vexation, had not changed for the worse, [and been] subjected to corruption and death.[9]

Yet in direct contrast, if not conflict, with this pervasive theme of the desirability of the soul's independence was Augustine's conviction, repeated over and over again in dispute with the Manichees, of the intrinsic goodness of the human body created by God. It is worth noting that even *On the Grandeur of the Soul* and *On Music* (the treatise from which the passages already quoted come) have passages speaking positively of the body.

> In view of our discussion, who can reasonably offer any complaint because it was given to the soul to move and manage the body, since an order of things so great and so divine could not be better linked together? Or who will think that we ought to inquire how the soul is affected in this mortal and frail body, since it is thrust together into death deservedly because of sin, but by virtue of [free will] it has the power to rise above the body?"[10]

> The body has nevertheless its own kind of beauty and by that beauty it appropriately commends the dignity of the

[9]*On Music* VI,iv.7.
[10]*Grandeur* 36.81.

soul, which deserves neither by punishment nor by sickness to be without the honour of some ornament.[11]

Later in his life (405-410) Augustine would argue that the body was not to be shunned [*fugiendum*] because the blessed in heaven will have bodies, eternally incorruptible, and that bodies, which in this life are "torments," will then be "ornaments."[12]

Although Augustine could not for many years relieve the intellectual tension between his conception of the ultimate good of the human person and his belief in the created goodness of the material world, he was able to approach the question of bodily resurrection through that other difficult tenet of faith, the Incarnation. That the Word had become man and was raised, and the resurrection of Christians are themes woven together in his writings in a variety of ways. On the most basic level, that which was for Christ a glory, a reward and evidence of his power,[13] is for the Christian a compelling aid to faith and virtuous living.

> Indeed, our belief in the resurrection of our Lord from the dead and his ascension into heaven sustains our faith with great hope. For this belief shows us forcibly how willingly he who had the power to take it up again laid down his life for us. What great confidence then inspires the hope of the faithful when they consider what great things he who is so great suffered for men who were not yet believers. When he is expected from heaven as the judge of the living and the dead, he strikes great fear into the negligent, with the result that they devote themselves to earnest effort and long for him by leading saintly lives, instead of dreading his coming because of their wicked lives.[14]

[11]*On Music* VI.iv.7.

[12]*Serm.* 241.vii.7.

[13]Cf. *Unfinished Commentary on the Epistle to the Romans* 5.1-5, 11-12.

[14]*On Christian Doctrine* I.xv.14 Cf. also *1 En. in Ps.* 29.10, *Against Fortunatus* 19.14, *Serm.* 316.8.

Augustine takes pains in his *Propositions from the Epistle to the Romans* and his *Unfinished Commentary on the Epistle to the Romans* to explain that it was not the mere fact of Christ's resurrection which predestined him to be the Son of God, but rather the resurrection's primal and initiating character which made him firstborn from the dead and head of the church:

> He was predestined Son of God and Lord of . . . David by the resurrection of the dead[15]

> For in the resurrection appears the power of Christ who died, so that it might be said: "predestined in power according to the Spirit of sanctification by the resurrection of the dead." Thereafter sanctification achieved new life, which is signified in our Lord's resurrection . . . The word order . . . could be such that we might connect 'by the resurrection of the dead' not to "the Spirit of sanctification" but to "he was predestined." The order then would be: "who was predestined by the resurrection of the dead," and interpolated into this order were the following words: "Son of God in power according to the Spirit of sanctification." This word order seems surer and better, so that Christ is the Son of David in weakness according to the flesh, but Son of God in power according to the Spirit of sanctification.[16]

> Moreover, Paul does not say that Christ was predestined by *his* resurrection *from* the dead, but "*the* resurrection *of* the dead." For his own resurrection does not show how he is the Son of God, and by this special and most outstanding worthiness the head of the Church, since others also will be raised from the dead. But he was predestined Son of God by a certain primacy of resurrection, since he himself was predestined by the resurrection

[15]*Commentary* 5.6. Quotations from the commentary and the propositions are taken from P.F. Landes, *Augustine on Romans* (Chico: Scholars' Press, 1982).

[16]*Commentary* 5.2,4-5.

of all the dead; that is, he was appointed to rise above and before the others, so that when Paul adds "the Son of God" to "predestined" this serves as proof of such great sublimity. For the Son of God alone was appropriately so predestined according to which he is also the head of the church, and for this reason Paul elsewhere calls him the first-born from the dead (Col 1:18).[17]

By the mid-390s Augustine had worked out a theology of Christ's death which identified the cross not only with the death of sinful desire, but also with the expunging of the generic guilt of humankind. Concurrently, he sees Christ's resurrection as a renewal of life, not only for himself, but for the Christian in the new life of sanctification. In the same writings on Romans we find this thought expressed:

For as the crucifixion of the old man was symbolized by the cross of the Lord, so the renewal of the new man was signified by the resurrection.[18]

Sanctification thereafter achieved new life, which is signified in our Lord's resurrection.[19]

And in a sermon preached in 400 he says:

Christ was crucified so that in his cross he might show forth the death of our old man, and he rose so that in his life he might show forth the newness of life.... His resurrection renews us.[20]

The renewal was not only, in Augustine's mind, a question of the power of Christ as archetype or example, although that notion is ever present,[21] but of a change in the believer's

[17]*Commentary* 5.11-12.

[18]*Propositions* 32.2.

[19]*Commentary* 5.2.

[20]*Serm.* 231.2.2. Cf. *Propositions* 32.2.

[21]Cf. e.g. *En. in Ps. 3.9, Commentary* 5.13, *En. in Ps. 148.16.*

status parallel to and completing that effected by the cross, a
further liberation from the power of the devil.

> Christ is said to have made a show of [the hostile powers]
> because in himself, our Head, he gave an example which
> will be fully realized in the liberation from the power of
> the devil of his whole body, the church, at the resurrec-
> tion.... [It is] an assured hope...already present and in
> our actual possession, our future life which is now ful-
> filled in our risen Head and Mediator, the man Jesus
> Christ.[22]

Augustine wrote and preached countless times that this
renewal of life is not automatic, but must be appropriated in
faith ("[while we are] in the flesh, faith in his resurrection
saves and justifies us"[23]), and that this life of faith constitutes the present reign of Christ and a foretaste of the
resurrection. He writes in *On Eighty-three Different Questions*:

> Christ will hand the kingdom over to God and the Father
> when through him the Father will be known by sight, for
> his kingdom consists of those in whom he now reigns
> through faith. In fact, in one sense Christ's kingdom
> means his divine power according to which every created
> thing is subject to him; and in another sense his kingdom
> means the church in respect to the faith which it has in
> him.[24]

The passage just quoted is implicitly anti-millenarian, and,
although there is some suggestion that Augustine tended
towards millenarianism in his early years as a Christian (for
example, in *Sermon* 259, usually dated to 393) later in *On*

[22]*Cont. Faust.* XIV.14.

[23]*De Trin.* II.xvii.298. Quotations from *De Trinitate* are taken from S.
McKenna, *Saint Augustine: The Trinity* (Washington: Catholic University of
America, 1963).

[24]*De Div Quest. LXXXIII* 69.4. Quotations is taken from D. Mosher, *Eighty-
three Different Questions.* (Washington. CA, 1977).

the Trinity he explicitly repudiates the expectation of an interim reign of Christ.

> Nor may we hold that Christ shall so deliver the kingdom to God and the Father as to deprive himself of it, as some Christians have even believed.... What then is the meaning of "when he shall deliver the kingdom to God and the Father?" Perhaps that God the Father does not have the kingdom at the present time? No, but that the man Christ Jesus, the Mediator between God and men, reigns now among all the just who live by faith, and shall one day bring them to that sight, which the same apostle calls the vision "face to face." Therefore, to say "he shall deliver the kingdom to God and the Father," is the same as saying when he shall lead the believers to the contemplation of God and the Father.[25]

The various strands of Augustine's theology of resurrection to approximately the year 405 are brought together in a passage in book four of *On the Trinity*. In response to the question how the single death and resurrection of Christ affects the double death of human persons, he explains:

> The Savior applied his own single death to this double death of ours, and, to bring about our resurrection in both, he offered his one resurrection both as sacrament and type... In his one death (of the body, not of sin) and one resurrection (of the body) he harmonizes our double death and resurrection, his resurrection completing the mystery of our inner man and giving the example of our outer man. We should believe that he has risen and rise with him by faith.[26]

The notion of Christ's resurrection as not only symbol and model of human life renewed,[27] but also its anticipation,

---

[25] *De Trin.* I.viii.16.

[26] *De Trin.* IV,iii.6. Cf. also *Serm.* 362.20.23 and 21.24.

[27] *Serm.* 240.i.1; 362.10.

of course, brings to the fore the question of the nature of resurrection life and, particularly, of the resurrection body. There are countless assertions in Augustine's writings that he thought Christ's resurrection to have been a bodily one: he rose "in true flesh,"[28] in an earthly body changed into a spiritual body,[29] "in the substance of the flesh he had put aside,"[30] in a true body, "the flesh of which was healed when he rose."[31] Affirmations in themselves, however, tell us little more than that he accepted the church's teaching on the subject, very little about how, exactly, he envisaged the resurrection body. It is only fair to point out that he did not pretend to certainty on this point, that he, in fact, to some extent discouraged positive speculation.[32] Negatively he had less hesitation. He was unequivocal in stating that he did not, on the one hand, believe in the kind of resurrection in which the Jews were said to believe, that is in a future material life like that of this world.[33] But he denies, on the other hand, that the body would be changed into 'spirit.' As early as 393 he writes

> The Gentiles mostly ply us eagerly with the arguments of the philosophers who say that an earthly object cannot exist in heaven. They do not know our scriptures, or how it is written: "It is sown an animal body; it is raised a spiritual body." This does not mean that body is changed into spirit and becomes spirit. The spiritual body is understood as a body so subject to spirit that it may be suited to its celestial habitation[34]

And again, about fifteen years later:

[28] *Serm.* 214.iii.3 (391).
[29] *De Fide et Symbolo* 6.13 (393).
[30] *Serm.* 235.3.4 (400).
[31] *2 En. in Ps. 29.*12 (415).
[32] *Serm.* 362. 25.27, *Letter* 147.51.
[33] *Serm.* 362.15.18.
[34] *De F.S.* 6.13.

> "Spiritual body" does not mean "not a body" any more
> than "animated body" means "life". . . . "Spiritual body"
> means a body obeying the spirit.[35]

No writer of the patristic age tried harder than Augustine to
explain the mediating pauline phrase, 'spiritual body,' to
describe what changes the earthly body will undergo. The
core of every explanation is that the body will no longer be
an impediment to the vision of God. We have already seen
this idea hinted at ɪn 388 (cf. above, p. 166), and the nexɪ year
he explains to the Manichees that "in parauɪse ɪto which we
will restored by Christ] concupiscence will not war against
reason."[36] In 392 he described the body's future condition in
detail to Fortunatus.

> As long as we live according to the flesh. . . we are in the
> power of our habits, in such a way that we do not do what
> we wish to do. . . . [T]hat same flesh, which has tor-
> mented us so that we remained in sin, will be submissive
> to us in the resurrection and will cease to trouble us with
> the obstacles which it puts in the way of us observing the
> law of God and the divine commandments.[37]

Augustine's most extensive treatment of the resurrection,
prior to his writing *The City of God* is in *Sermon* 362,
preached about 410. In it, Augustine wrestles, as so many
had before him, with the text "flesh and blood cannot
inherit the kingdom of God," and develops the exegesis used
a hundred years earlier by Methodius to further his
argument.

> Your body does not possess anything, but your soul,
> through the body, possesses that which belongs to the
> body. If, therefore, the flesh resurrects in order not to

[35]*Serm.* 242.8.11.

[36]*On Genesis against the Manichees* II.xii.16.

[37]*Fortunatus* 22. Cf. Also *Gen.Litt* VI.xix.30, xxiv.35, *Serm.* 362.7.7, 10.10.

possess but to be possessed, not to have but to be had, what wonder then if flesh and blood cannot possess the kingdom, since they will certainly be possessed by another. . . . In so far as we will be resurrected, it is not we whom the flesh carries, it is we who will carry it. If we carry it, we will possess it; if we will possess it, we will not be possessed by it; for we are freed from the judgement of the demon; we are of the kingdom of God. In this sense this flesh and blood do not possess the kingdom of God.[38]

Later in the sermon, commenting on 1 Corinthians 15:487-49 ("Such as is the heavenly, such also are they that are heavenly" and "Therefore as we have borne the image of the earthly, let us bear also the image of the heavenly"), he approaches the text more conventionally, in terms of his understanding of 'spiritual body'.

The Apostle wants us to believe that our resurrected life will not be like the corruptible which preceded it, and he adds immediately: "This also I declare to you brothers, that flesh and blood cannot possess the heritage of the kingdom of God." And he also wishes to explain why he said "flesh" and "blood," because it is not the nature of the body itself, but corruption which will no longer be. For a body wihout corruption cannot properly be said to be flesh and blood; it is simply a body. For if it is flesh, it is corruptible and mortal; if it no longer dies, it is no longer corruptible; therefore without corruption, although the form remains, it is no longer flesh but body; if it is said to be flesh, it is no longer said properly, but by a kind of analogy.[39]

To have the form of a body, without the flesh of corruption, means for Augustine (as it did for Macrina), that none of the 'acts of the flesh' (eating, drinking, begetting and

---

[38]*Serm.*362.13.14. Quotations from this sermon are taken from J.A. Mourant, *Augustine on Immortality* (Villanova: Augustinian Institute, 1969), appendix.

[39]*Serm.* 362.xv.17.

bearing children) will have a place in heaven. Human beings will be "like the angels of God."[40]

> [The heavenly body] will be called a body and it can be called a celestial body. The same thing is said by the Apostle when he distinguishes between bodies: "All flesh is not the same flesh: but one is the flesh of men, another of beasts, another of birds, another of fishes. And there are bodies celestial and bodies terrestrial" (1 Cor 15:39-40). However, he certainly would not say celestial flesh; although bodies may be said to be flesh but only earthly bodies. For all flesh is body; but not every body is flesh.[41]

But, after all his attempts at explanation, Augustine is driven to say:

> Now then, brothers, one ought not to inquire with a perverse kind of subtlety what the form of the body will be after the resurrection, what stature, what movement, what gait it will have. It is sufficient for you to know that your flesh resurrects in that form in which the Lord appeared, that is, in the human form. . . . That which was made manifest in Him as the Head is expected for the members; on this foundation is revealed that edifice constructed by our faith which will be perfected afterward through sight.[42]

It was said at the beginning of this chapter that Augustine's conviction that eternal human happiness will lie in the intellectual contemplation of divine Truth was in tension with his acceptance of the christian doctrine of the resurrection of the body. Certainly his distinction between flesh and body in dealing with that resurrection was an attempt to resolve this tension. Nevertheless, no matter how spiritual

[40]*Serm.* 362.15.18.
[41]*Serm.* 362.xviii.21.
[42]*Serm.* 362.25.27.

he envisages the risen body to be, he can not bring himself to assert that the eyes of the spiritual body had a positive role to play in the human being's sight of God; the 'sight' alluded to in the last passage quoted was not bodily sight. A number of texts, both earlier and later than *Sermon* 362, make this point clear. Writing to Paulina in 413 on the vision of God (in *Letter* 147, which is really a treatise), Augustine says:

> When you asked me to write you something lengthy and detailed about the invisible God and whether He can be seen by bodily eyes, I could not refuse lest I affront your holy zeal....But...it is such a deep subject that it becomes more difficult the more one thinks about it—not so much in what is to be thought and said of it, but in the method of persuasion to be used with those who hold contrary opinions.[43]

The contrary-minded are clearly those who believe that the risen body will be corporeal and that God will, therefore, be seen materially.[44] Augustine begins his argument by discussing the vision of God in the present life:

> We believe that God is seen in the present life, but do we believe that we see Him with our bodily eyes, as we see the sun, or with the gaze of the mind, as everyone sees himself inwardly, when he sees himself living, wishing, seeking, knowing, or not knowing?... to look upon those things which...are beheld by the mind...you do not use your bodily eyes, nor do you perceive or look for any part of space through which your gaze may travel in order to attain the sight of these things.[45]

The distinction between the gaze of the bodily eyes and that of the mind is vital to his argument, Augustine tells Paulina,

---

[43]*Letter* 147.1. Quotations from this letter are taken from W. Parsons, *St. Augustine's Letters* (New York: Fathers of the Church, 1953), vol. 3, 131-64.

[44]*Letter* 147.49.

[45]*Letter* 147.3.

because there are some who do not recognize the existence of the latter, and so think that anything but the corporeal can be known only be faith, "that the...act which we call belief is the only act of the mind when it looks upon something."[46] Augustine dismisses such a position with a reminder that the activity of memory is like faith in seeing mentally what is not present to our senses.[47]

Working to reconcile "Blessed are the clean of heart, for they shall see God" (Mt 5:8) and "No man has seen God at any time" (1 Jn 3:2), Augustine turns to Ambrose's commentary on Luke's gospel for help, and he quotes from Ambrose in writing to Paulina.

> "Therefore, 'no one has seen God at any time,' because no one hath beheld that fullness of the divinity which dwells in God; no one has experienced it with mind or eyes, for the word 'seen' is to be referred to both. Finally when [John] adds, 'the only-begotten Son himself, he hath declared him,' it is the sight of minds rather than of eyes which is described.... Is it any wonder that the Lord is not seen in the present world except when He wills? Even in the resurrection itself it is not easy to see God, except for the clean of heart."[48]

As he continues the treatise, Augustine interprets and adds to Ambrose's words.

> Therefore, God is invisible by nature, and not only the Father, but also the Trinity itself, one God, and because He is not only invisible but also unchangeable, He appears to whom He wills, and under the aspect that He wills, so that His invisible and unchangeable nature may remain wholly within Himself. But the longing of the truly devout soul, by which they desire to see God and

---

[46]*Letter* 147. 6. Cf. also 10.

[47]*Letter* 147.8.

[48]*Letter* 147.18.

burn with eager love for Him, is not enkindled, I think, by desire to see that aspect under which He appears as He wills, but which is not Himself; they long for the substance by which He is what He is.[49]

Augustine was adamant in maintaining his position that only the clean of heart will see God, and he again quotes Ambrose:

"God is not seen in any locality, but in the clean heart, that is, He is not sought by bodily eyes, nor limited by our sight"[50]

A further argument for the inaccessibility of God to the eyes of even the risen body is the general one of the invisibility of all spiritual natures:

Since something of us is visible, like the body, and something invisible, like the interior man, and since the best part of us, that is, the mind and intelligence, is invisible to the eyes of the body, how shall that which is better than the best part of us be visible to our lower part?[51]

There will be something for the bodily eyes to see in the risen life, Augustine agreed, but he does not specify in this letter what that will be: "Let this be enough to say."[52] It will not be the fulness of God. Augustine reiterated this point tirelessly. In *On the Trinity*, he insists that Wisdom is an incorporeal substance and a light in which those things are seen which are not seen with carnal eyes.[53] *Letter* 92 (408) argues against those "who say that in the future life we shall see God with bodily sight, that even the 'wicked will see,'"[54]

[49] *Letter* 147. 47. Cf. also 28.
[50] *Letter* 147.20.
[51] *Letter* 147.45.
[52] *Letter* 147.54
[53] *Trinity* XV.8.
[54] *Letter* 92.4.

and *Letter* 148, to Fortunatianus in 413, repeats many of the arguments of *Letter* 147 (and appeals as well to the authority of Jerome, Athanasius and Gregory).

> [T]he eyes of this body can see nothing but corporeal objects.... [If] our bodies are going to be changed into something so unlike themselves that they will have eyes capable of seeing that substance which is not distributed through portions of space, nor limited by it... but, everywhere incorporeally wholly present, these bodies will be something very different. They will not be different merely through the removal of mortality, corruption and the weight of matter, but they will be changed in some way into the very quality of the mind itself, if they are going to be able to see in a way which will be granted to the mind then, but which is not granted even to the mind at present.[55]

It is interesting that in these two letters to Paulina and Fortunatus Augustine seems less certain than he had earlier been that the risen body will not be a spirit. In the first letter, the notion that the risen body "puts off not only its mortal and corruptible state, but even the very act of being a body, and becomes a spirit" is called only "contrary to custom";[56] and in the second he writes:

> Concerning the spiritual body which we will have at the resurrection...: whether it will be merged into the simplicity of the soul so that the whole man becomes spirit, or whether, as I think more likely, but have not sufficient certitude to affirm, it will become a body so spiritual that it may be called spiritual because of some indescribable facility it will have, while retaining the corporeal substance which can have life and consciousness only through the soul which makes use of it... on these mat-

[55] *Letter* 148.2-3.
[56] *Letter* 147-51.

ters I confess that I have not yet read anything which I think satisfactory either to learn or to teach.[57]

Nevertheless, about a year later in *On the Literal Interpretation of Genesis*, Augustine tackles the subject again.

But why must the spirits of the departed be reunited with their bodies in the resurrection, if they can be admitted to the supreme beatitude without their bodies? This is a problem that may trouble some, but it is too difficult to be answered with complete satisfaction in this essay. There should, be no doubt that a man's mind, when it is carried out of the senses of the flesh in ecstasy, or when after death it has departed from the flesh, is unable to see the immutable essence of God just as the holy angels see it, even though it has passed beyond the likenesses of corporeal things. This may be because of some mysterious reason or simply because of the fact that it possesses a kind of natural appetite for managing the body. By reason of this appetite it is somehow hindered from going on with all its force to the highest heaven, long as it is not joined with the body, for it is in managing the body that this appetite is satisfied.

Moreover, if the body is such that the management of it is difficult and burdensome, as is the case with this corruptible flesh, which is a load upon the soul (coming as it does from a fallen race), the mind is much more readily turned away from the vision of the highest heaven. Hence it must necessarily be carried out of the senses of the flesh in order to be granted this vision as far as it is able. Accordingly, when the soul is made equal to the angels and receives again this body, no longer a natural body but a spiritual one because of the transformation that is to be, it will have the perfect measure of its being, obeying and commanding, vivified and vivifying with such a wonderful ease that what once was its burden will be its glory.

[57]*Letter 148.5.*

Then, indeed, there will be the three kinds of vision of
which we have been speaking, but no error will induce us
to mistake one thing for another, either in regard to
corporeal objects or in regard to spiritual objects, or especially in regard to intellectual objects. There will be joy
in the things of the intellect, and they will be far more
luminously present to the soul than the corporeal forms
that now surround us, which we perceive through the
senses of our body. Yet many are now so absorbed in these
material forms that they judge them to be the only ones,
and they think that anything of a different order is simply
nonexistent. But, although the corporeal world is more
obvious, wise men live in the midst of it, clinging with
greater surety to the world beyond bodily forms and
beyond the likenesses of bodies, the world which they see
with the intellect according to their measure, although
they are not able to behold it in the mind so vividly as they
do these other objects with the senses of the body.[58]

Augustine's most extensive treatment of the fate of
human persons (and the one he considered the best[59]) is
found in the final books of *The City of God*. It is largely a
reiteration of the positions expressed in his earlier
writings—although with one important difference. In the
context of "the appointed destinies of both cities, the earthly
and the heavenly," Augustine asks again what is the state in
which good "is brought to complete perfection" and "the
final end of the harmful course we take under [evil's] gui-
dance?"[60] Discarding as inadequate various philosophical
understandings of the human person and of ultimate human
good and evil, Augustine, as always, locates both ultimate
good and ultimate evil in eternity, and expresses salvation
initially in this treatise as freedom from the evils of temporal
life.

---

[58]*De Gen. Ad Litt.* XII 35-36. Translation taken from J.H. Taylor, trans. and
annot. *The Literal Meaning of Genesis*, New York: Newman Press, 1982, 228-30.

[59]*Retractions* I.16.

[60]*The City of God* XIX.1.

> For we are among those evils, which we ought patiently
> to endure until we arrive among those goods where
> nothing will be lacking to provide us ineffable delight,
> nor will there now be anything that we are obliged to
> endure.[61]

Book twenty-one sees a new approach to demonstrating a
bodily life in eternity. Augustine begins with the corporeal
punishment of the damned:

> Since in both cases there will be bodies, and it seems
> harder to believe that bodies last on in eternal torment
> than that they continue to exist in eternal happiness
> without any pain, it follows that, once I have proved that
> such punishment is not incredible, my task will be much
> lightened in that the future corporeal immortality of the
> saints, in a life free from every vexation, will much more
> easily win assent.[62]

The question Augustine is addressing here is how a body
could endlessly survive the pain and trauma of fire. He is
convinced that the fire is not figurative, but material,[63] and
that it will be eternal because of the seriousness of the primal
sin.[64] He disagrees with those who say that none will be
condemned,[65] and with Origen's "excessive mercifulness" in
positing the eventual reconciliation of the devil.[66] With the
help of several examples, he points out that pain does not
inevitably bring death,[67] but is in fact a sign of life, not
death.[68] Furthermore, he argues, the conviction that a body

[61]*City* XIX.4.
[62]*City* XIX.1.
[63]*City* XXI.3.
[64]*City* XXI.12.
[65]*City* XXI.17.
[66]*City* XXI.17.
[67]*City* XXI.2.
[68]*City* XXI.3.

which can feel pain can—and eventually must—die is based on our present bodily perceptions and experience, and may not apply in the life to come.[69] Pain causes death when it causes the soul to retreat from the body, "but at that time the soul will be knit to such a body and with such a knot, that the bond will no more be broken by pain than it will be loosened by any lapse of time."[70]

He continues:

> The first death thrusts the soul from the body against its will, the second death holds it fast in its body against its will. What is shared by both kinds of death is this, that the soul must have dealt to it by its body what it does not choose to suffer.[71]

The fate of the damned is thus precisely the opposite of that of the blessed, who will not be at the mercy of their bodies.

Book twenty-two deals with the life of the blessed in heaven, and begins with another discussion of the possibility of the body sharing that life. The philosophers say that "nature would not have anything which is formed of earth dwell anywhere except on earth,"[72] and the same argument is repeated a little later in terms of the weight of the elements: earth, water, air and heaven.[73] Augustine meets this argument with two of his own, the first appealing to the power of God, the second to the widespread faith in Christ's resurrection. His first point is that it is not more unnatural to have bodies in heaven than to have souls joined to bodies.

> For why are we not more amazed that incorporeal spirits, which are better than even heavenly bodies, are bound to

---

[69]*City XXI.3.*
[70]*City* XXI.3,
[71]*City* XXI.3.
[72]*City* XXII.4.
[73]*City* XXII.11.

earthly bodies, than that earthly bodies will be lifted up to a home which, although heavenly, is nevertheless corporeal? Is it not because we are wont to see the one marvel daily, and in fact are that marvel ourselves, but are not yet that other thing, nor have we ever hitherto seen it?[74]

He appeals again to the power of God with a different and material illustration.

[The philosophers' arguments are the sort] whereby human weakness, a prey to vanity, contradicts the omnipotence of God! What business [, they say,] have all these earthly bodies in the air, when the air is third from the earth? Cannot he who with feathers and wings gave lightness to the earthly bodies of birds, that they might soar in the air, bestow a special power on the bodies of men, when he makes them immortal, that will enable them to dwell even in the highest heaven?[75]

This same motif—that present human knowledge does not exhaust all possibilities—is applied to faith in the resurrection of Christ.

[In earlier ages] the human mind could not have believed in the resurrection of Christ in the flesh and his ascension to heaven, but would have mocked at the story, closed their ears, and rejected it from their hearts as impossible, if the possibility and the fact had not been demonstrated by the divinity of Truth itself, and by the truth of Divinity, as well as by the miraculous signs that confirmed the fact.[76]

Earlier positive statements of Augustine's concerning the human body have been cited, but none compares with the

[74]*City* XXII.4.
[75]*City* XXII.11.
[76]*City* XXII.7.

praise lavished on it in *The City of God*. Human fecundity, propagation, intelligence and possible conformation to the divine image are presented as among the good things of earthly life. The body is lauded for the harmony of its parts, for its utility and, more importantly, for its beauty. Even in this life.

> are not the sense organs and other members so arranged in it, and the appearance, shape and stature of the whole body so adapted that it shows clearly that it was designed to serve a rational soul?[77]

And hereafter, "The time will come when we shall enjoy nothing but one another's beauty without any lust."[78]

Opposing the platonists, Augustine returns to the theme of the incorruptible body.

> So, in order to be happy, souls need not flee from every kind of body [as they taught], but must receive an incorruptible body. And in what incorruptible body will they more fittingly rejoice than in the one in which they groaned while it was corruptible?[79]

For the first time we find Augustine replying to the objections which were so familiar to earlier apologists. What size will the risen body be? What becomes of nail and hair cuttings? What about bodies dispersed by fire, shipwreck and decay? All these materials will be gathered and renewed as human flesh, is his response.[80] He uses (as had Methodius) the analogy of a statue which is melted down and recast, illnesses and deformities cured.[81] Bodies will be beautiful and "will shine like the sun"[82] and "each will

[77]*City* XXII.24.
[78]*City* XXII.24.
[79]*City* XXII.26.
[80]*City* XXII.12.
[81]*City* XXII.19.
[82]*City* XXII.19.

receive his own measure," a measure Augustine thought would be that of the age and strength reached by Christ.[83]

That Augustine was now concerned with questions of this kind indicates both the extent to which *The City of God* was written to be read by pagans, and (more importantly) his own increased consciousness of the bitterness of the controversies surrounding the resurrection body.[84] Neither, however, deflected him from his own vision of the afterlife. Despite the criticisms of Origen mentioned above, Augustine's attitude was much closer to his than to that of Methodius. "To attain to the perfect man" had for him little to do with the state of the risen body and everything to do with coming to a full knowledge of the Son of God.[85] Nothing more strongly illustrates his conviction that such knowledge is entirely intellectual and spiritual, than his refusal—even in the context just described, when he must have been under a certain pressure to stress the materiality of the risen body—to abandon the position he had held for thirty years and to say that God will be seen with corporeal eyes.

The question is thrashed out in chapter twenty-nine of this last book of *The City of God*, and what he does not say is as informative as what he does. What will be the activity of the saints in their immortal and spiritual bodies? Augustine admits that he does not know

> [W]hat that activity, or rather, that peace and rest, will be like, for I have never experienced it through my bodily senses. And if I should say that I have perceived it in my mind or understanding, what is our understanding in comparison with that excellence?[86]

The blessed will see God in the body, but it is "no easy

---

[83]*City* XXII.15.

[84]If evidence were needed that Augustine knew of the controversies focusing on Origen's theories of the resurrection, the references in book XXI.17 and in *Ep.* 148.6f would provide it.

[85]*City* XXII.18.

[86]*City* XXII.29.

question" whether that sight will be by means of bodily eyes. The words of John ("but now my eye sees thee," 42:5) and of Paul ("face to face," 1 Cor 13:12) notwithstanding, Augustine insists that the eyes which will see God will need very different powers from those of corporeal eyes.[87] Yet will the power of the spiritual body be so great that God, who is Spirit, will be able to be seen by a body?[88] In the the end, Augustine cannot bring himself to say that the eyes of the body will see divine Truth in its essence, and he points out that the christian scriptures do not, in fact, teach such a doctrine. He offers instead a theory that is noteworthy for what it does and does not grant to those who assert that the risen body will be corporeal. The risen bodies of the just will be seen, and those bodies will mediate the sight of God to others, not the sight of the divine nature, but that of God's presence and rule:

> [W]e shall see the corporeal bodies of the new heaven and the new earth in such a way that, wherever we turn our eyes, we shall, through our bodies that we are wearing and plainly seeing, enjoy with perfect clarity the vision of the sight of God everywhere present and ruling all things, even material things. It will not be as it is now, when the invisible things of God are seen and understood through the things which have been made, in a mirror dimly and in part.[89]

> Either, therefore, God will be seen by means of those eyes because they in their excellence will have something similar to mind by which even an incorporeal nature is discerned—but that is difficult or impossible to illustrate by any example or testimony of the divine writings—or else, which is easier to understand, God will be so known by us and so present to our eyes that by means of the spirit he will be seen by each of us in each of us, seen by each in

[87]*City* XXII.29.
[88]*City* XXII.29.
[89]*City* XXII.29.

his neighbour and in himself, seen in the new heaven and the new earth and in every creature which will then exist.[90]

It is remarkable that nowhere in this, his most thorough discussion of life after death, does Augustine expound the conviction he had held for thirty years that ultimate human happiness will lie in the eternal contemplation of divine Truth, "face to face." The reason, as I have suggested above, was probably the audience, pagan and christian, to which it was directed; Augustine had always saved his description of that contemplation for his kindred spirits. He had certainly not abandoned his hope. In the later part of *On the Trinity* in a reference to John 15:5, ("...when he appears, we shall be like to him, for we shall see him just as he is"), Augustine offers two interpretations:

> Hence, it is clear that the full likeness to God will then be realized in this image of God when it shall receive the full vision of him. And yet it is also possible to see in these words of John the Apostle a reference to the immortality of the body. For in this, too, we shall be like God, but only the Son, because he alone in the Trinity took a body, in which he died, rose again, and which he brought to higher things.
> ...That is to say, let us who were mortal according to Adam hold fast to this with a true faith and with a certain and firm hope that we shall be immortal according to Christ.[91]

And finally:

> Therefore, let us now seek the Trinity...in the perfect contemplation of which the blessed life, which is none other than eternal life, is promised to us.[92]

[90]*City* XXII.29.
[91]De Trin. XIV.xviii.24.
[92]*De Trin.* XV.iv.6.

Suggested Readings

I. Background

Mildenberger, F. "Auferstehung" in *Theologische Realen-zyklopadie* (Berlin/New York: Walter de Gruyter, 1979) IV, 441-575.

Bevan, E. *The Hope of a World to Come underlying Judaism and Christianity* (London: Allen and Unwin, 1930).

Brandon, S.G.F. *The Judgement of the Dead. An Historical and Comparative Study of the Idea of a Postmortem judgement in the Major Religions* (London: Weidenfeld and Nicolson, 1967).

Charles, R.H. *A Critical History of the Doctrine of a Future Life in Israel, Judaism and Christianity* (London: A. and C. Black, 1899, republished with a new title and introduction, New York: Schocken Books, 1963).

Hick, J. *Death and Eternal Life* (London: Collins, 1976).

Stendhal, K. ed. *Immortality and Resurrection* (New York: Macmillan, 1965).

Zaehner, R.C. *The Teachings of the Magi*. London: George, Allen and Unwin, 1956.

II. New Testament

Bruce, F.F. "Paul's changing view of after-death," *Theology Digest* 21 (Spring 1973), 8-11.

Cornelis, H. ed. *La Resurrection de la chair* (Paris: Editions du Cerf, 1962).

Evans, C.F. *Resurrection and the New Testament* (London: SCM, 1970).

Sider, R.J. "The Pauline Conception of the Resurrection Body in 1 Corinthians XV", *New Testament Studies* 21 (1974-75), 428-39.

Stanley, D.M. *Christ's Resurrection in Pauline Soteriology* (Rome: Pontical Biblical Institute, 1961).

III. General Patristic

Altermath, F. *Du corps psychique au corps spirituel. Interpretation de I Cor 15:35-49 par les auteurs chretiens des quatre premiers siecles* [=Beitrage zur Geschichte des biblischen Exegese, 18] (Tübingen: JCB Mohr, 1977).

Davies, J.G. "Factors Leading to the Emergence of Belief in the Resurrection of the Flesh," *Journal of Theological Studies*, n.s. 23 (1972), 448-55.

Eijk, A.H.C. van, *La resurrection des morts dans les Peres apostoliques*. Paris: Beauchesne, 1974.

Fischer, J.A. *Studien zum Todesgedanken im der alten Kirche* (Munchen, M. Hueber, 1954).

Grant, R.M. "The resurrection of the Body," *Journal of Religion* 27 (1948), 120-30, 188-208.

Kretschmar, G. "Auferstenhung des Fleisches: Zur Fruhgeschichte einer theologischen Lehrformel," *Leben an-*

gesichts des Todes [Festschrift H. Thielicke] (Tübingen, J.C.B. Mohr, 1968).

Pelikan, J. *The Shape of Death: Life, Death and Immortality in the Early Fathers* (New York: Abingdon, 1961).

Prestige, L. "Hades in the Greek Fathers," *Journal of Theological Studies* 24 (1923), 476-85.

Refoule, F. "Immortalite de l' ame et resurrection de la chair," *Rev. de l 'Hist. des Religions* 441 (1963), 11-52.

Wolfson, H.A. "Immortality and resurrection in the philosophy of the Church Fathers," *Religious Philosophy* (Cambridge, Mass., Harvard, 1961).

IV. Particular writers of the Patristic Age

Armantage, J. "The Best of Both Worlds: Origen's Views on Religion and Resurrection," *Origeniana* (Universita di Bari, 1975), 339-47.

Barnard, L.W. "Athenagoras' *De Resurrectione*. The Background and Theology of a Second Century Treatise on the Resurrecion," *Studia Theologica* 30 (1976), 1-42.

——————————. "Justin Martyr's Eschatology," *Vigiliae Christianae* 19 (1965), 86-98.

Chadwick, H. "Origen, Celsus and the Resurrection of the Body," *Harvard Theological Review* 41 (1948), 83-102.

Crouzel, H. "Les critiques adressees par Methode et ses contemporains a la doctrine origenienne du corps ressuscite," *Gregorianum* 53 (1972), 679-716.

Danielou, J. "La Resurrection des corps chez Gregoire de Nysse," *Vigiliae Christianae* 7 (1953), 154-70.

Evans, E. *Tertullian's Treatise on the Resurrection* (London: SPCK, 1960).

Lienhard, J.T. "The exegesis of 1 Cor 15:24-28 from Marcellus of Ancyra to Theodoret of Cyrus," *Vigilia Christiana* 37 (1983), 340-59.

Mossay, J. *La mort et l' au-dela dans S. Gregoire de Nanziane* (Louvain: Bibliotheque de l' Universite, 1966).

O'Hagan, A. *Material Re-creation in the Apostolic Fathers* [=TU 100] (Berlin: Akademie-Verlag, 1968).

Rousseau, A. "L' eternite des peines de l'enfer et l' immortalite naturelle de l' ame selon S. Irenee," *Nouvelle Revue Theologique* 99 (1977), 834-64.

Studer, B. "La resurrection de Jesus d' apres le *Peri Archon' d'Origene*," Augustinianum 1 B (1978), 279-309.

General Index

Adam, 30, 34, 81, 110-111, 116, 164.
afterlife, expectation of, (1) in pagan antiquity, 12-13, 65, 71; (2) in Israelite religion, 16-24; in the New Testament, 13, 25-35.
Ambrose, 178.
Armantage, J., 137.
Athanasius, 180.
Athenagoras, 73-81.
Augustine, 59,164-189.

Babcock, W., 164.
Barnabas, 36, 38, 53-55.
Barnard, L. W., 58, 64, 73, 82.
Basil of Caesarea, 143, 149, 153, 157.
Benoit, P., 15.
Brandon, S. G. F., 12, 20-21.
Brown, R. E., 34.
Browne, C. G., 160.
Burns, J. P., 164.
Butterworth, G.W., 124.

Caesar (brother of Gregory of Nazianzus), 159-60.
Callahan, V. W., 150.
Chadwick, H. C., 116, 122, 124, 131.
chain consumption, theory of, 74-75, 84, 133, 186.
Charles, R. H., 21.
Clark, N., 29, 33, 34.
Clark, W. R., 138.

Clement of Alexandria, 114-122.
Clement of Rome, 36, 38-42, 49.
contemplation (of God after death), 70, 77, 155-156, 165, 176-189.
covenants (Old Testament), 15-18.
Croalto, S., 12.
Crouzel, H., 142.

Daniel (book of), 23.
Davies, J. G., 37-38, 100.
death, (1) in general, 11, 12, 79; (2) in Old Testament, 15-19; (3) in christian tradition, (a) as a result of Adam's sin, 30, 34, 36, 61, 70, 72, 83, 104, 115, 122, 164; (b) overcome by Christ's death, 11, 13, 30, 32, 34, 43, 49, 54, 116, 161, 170, 172.
Dechow, J. F., 144.
Deferrari, R. J., 157.
Demetrius, bishop, 123.
Dennis, J. T., 147.
Denzinger, H., 122.
Devreese, R., 161.
Didache, 37-38, 45-46, 53.
doceticism, 36-37, 49, 52, 80, 100-101, 118.
Dodd, C. H., 37.
Douglas, M., 38.
Dubarle, A. -M., 16, 25.
Dunne, J. S., 11.
Duval, Y. -M., 137.

Scripture Index